The Pursuit of Attention

The Pursuit of Attention
The Pursuit of Attention
The Pursuit of Attention

The Pursuit of Attention

Power and Ego in Everyday Life

Power and Ego in Everyday Life
Power and Ego in Everyday Life
Power and Ego in Everyday Life

Second Edition

Charles Derber

OXFORD
UNIVERSITY PRESS

2000

OXFORD

UNIVERSITY PRESS

Oxford   New York

Athens   Auckland   Bangkok   Bogotá   Buenos Aires   Calcutta
Cape Town   Chennai   Dar es Salaam   Delhi   Florence   Hong Kong   Istanbul
Karachi   Kuala Lumpur   Madrid   Melbourne   Mexico City   Mumbai
Nairobi   Paris   São Paulo   Singapore   Taipei   Tokyo   Toronto   Warsaw

and associated companies in
Berlin   Ibadan

First published by G.K. Hall & Co., Boston,
and in paperback by Schenkman Publishing Co., Cambridge, Massachusetts, 1979.

First issued as an Oxford University Press paperback,
New York, 1983

Published by Oxford University Press, Inc.
198 Madison Avenue, New York, New York 10016

Oxford is a registered trademark of Oxford University Press

Library of Congress Cataloging-in-Publication Data
Derber, Charles.
The pursuit of attention : power and ego in everyday life / Charles Derber.—2nd ed.
p. cm.
Includes bibliographical references and index.
ISBN 0-19-5135504— ISBN 0-19-513549-0 (pbk.)
1. Interpersonal relations. 2. Social interaction.
3. Individualism. 4. Social status.
5. Power (Social sciences) I. Title.
HM1106.D47 2000
302—dc21   99-056755

Book design by Adam B. Bohannon

2 4 6 8 9 7 5 3
Printed in the United States of America

To the memory of Morrie Schwartz
for the lessons in living
and the loving attention
that made this work possible

If I am not for myself, who will be for me?
But if I am for myself only, what am I?
And if not now, when?
—Hillel

…left remaining (is) no other nexus between
man and man than naked self-interest…
—Marx

Contents

Acknowledgments

I would be derelict if I did not acknowledge the intellectual influence of those whose critical work on individualism and class—Erich Fromm, Philip Slater, Richard Sennett, Jack Seeley, Ivan Illich, Robert Coles, and Christopher Lasch—so greatly stimulated my own thinking. Slater, Sennett, Seeley, Illich, and Coles all read and commented on the manuscript at various stages of its development, and I am grateful for their encouragement.

An author requires more than his share of personal attention to complete his task. I have been blessed with loving and intellectually challenging parents always supportive of my endeavors as well as many generous relatives and friends who have borne with me during periods of obsession and encouraged me in times of hesitancy and uncertainty. Those especially burdened, who offered both intellectual and emotional inspiration, include Brian McLauglin, Paul Weckstein, Barbara Zimbel, Yale Magrass, Dick Flacks, Bruce and Edie Weitzmann-Maddi, Ann Cordilia, and Morrie Schwartz.

I want to thank Elda Rotor at Oxford for championing a new edition of this book, and responding attentively at every new phase. My colleagues David Karp and John Williamson offered encouragement and insights for my new draft. And Elena Kolesnikova, as always, sustained me intellectually and emotionally throughout the new work.

Introduction to the Second Edition

One evening as I was coming out of a theater in New York City, I suddenly saw the Oscar-winning movie star Marisa Tomei. I could not take my eyes off her. I moved excitedly to get as close a look as possible, but I had to crane my neck because a gathering crowd of onlookers were scrambling to get their own close-up view. It wasn't her beauty that drew our rapt attention. It was the quivering sense of a larger-than-life moment, up-close and personal with a celebrity. I was surprised and a bit embarrassed by the force of my desire to drink in her presence.

If attention is a prize, then Tomei is certainly one of the winners, as are movie stars and celebrities in general. In the 1999 film *Notting Hill* Julia Roberts plays a celebrity actress who turns the star-struck people she meets into bowls of quivering jello. Although Roberts plays a modest star with ordinary qualities, people simply cannot take their eyes off her, overwhelmed just to be in her company and thrilled to touch her hand or clothes.

A celebrity is a person whose simple presence commands instant and overwhelming attention. Stars such as Tomei or Roberts don't have to do anything to get our attention; they control it simply by allowing themselves to be seen. Most of us get less electrifying and less positive attention, and we have to pursue it more vigorously and content ourselves with far less. Some of us get little attention from anyone. The opposite of a celebrity is someone who is invisible and can not get attention no matter what he or she does.

In the first edition of this book, I argued that the pursuit of attention is a window into the soul of our culture and that the competition for attention is one of the key contests of social life. I proposed that attention plays a role in social interaction as does money in the economy: people hunger for it and suffer terribly from its deprivation; many compete subtly but fiercely to get it; and it is one of the social badges of prestige and success.

By examining how people seek attention and analyzing who gets it, we can garner some important truths about ourselves and our society. The competition for attention has become a mirror of larger pathologies, reflecting broader and destructive forms of competition and egoism in American life. But there is nothing inherently corrupting or egoistic about the process of exchanging attention, and in some cultures, including many families and subcultures within our own society, it reflects generosity and love.

The pursuit of attention is now emerging as one of the electric organizing principles of American life. Not only are people pursuing attention in new ways, but there is evidence that we have begun to restructure our culture—including even our politics and economy—around the idea of attention as a glittering ultimate recognition and reward. Celebrities are the icons, but the pursuit of attention is now being diffused and institutionalized, hardwired into our beings through new systems of media, business, and technology, and fueled by new, aching deprivations that prey on our psyches. The result is a spreading virus of prosaic but dehumanizing behavior that subtly alienates us from one another and turns daily interaction into a veiled competition for recognition and respect.

The tragedy of Princess Diana—pursued all her adult life by merciless photographers—clearly shows that too much unwanted attention can be a terrible plague, and many celebrities don disguises in public to maintain some privacy. The pursuit of attention is discriminating even for celebrities, and many ordinary people shun center stage both in public and private. But millions of us—and there are tantalizing hints that the numbers are growing—use social relations as an opportunity to call attention to ourselves, a dynamic that can be seen as a democratization of celebrity. Few of us expect to become celebrities and many of us feel some distance or even disdain for the mania about celebrity in America. But the essence of celebrity is the capacity to attract a great deal of attention when we want it and to excite others by our very presence, and that is something that all of us can try to do in our own very different ways.[1]

Celebrities pursue and attract mass public attention, notably on TV and in the media. Many ordinary Americans—including some of us repelled by the sheer excess and obsessive media attention showered on celebrities—are attention-seekers, but on a much smaller and more private stage. While the more ambitious use new technology or professional accomplishments to compete for media attention, many of the rest of us participate in a far less glamorous version of the pursuit, such as when we simply talk about ourselves in conversation rather than listen to others. Such routine forms of attention-seeking are hardly ever the subject of either tabloid or scholarly discussion and are typically cloaked in exquisite rituals of civility. But they now infect much of our workplace or family interaction and have a deep and sometimes debilitating effect on our everyday lives.

Four emerging trends illustrate the evolution of our attention-pursuing culture. One is the spreading influence of a fashion industry that has turned supermodels into celebrities rivaling movie stars; it is breeding a new kind of preoccupation with bodily image, beauty, and fashion that affects the way millions of ordinary Americans seek attention, and it threatens now to turn much of ordinary social interaction into the manufacture and manipulation of image. Popular TV channels such as E!, the Entertainment cable channel, devote endless programming to showing sexy supermodels on fashion runways. The supermodels command the concentrated attention of many millions of people, who are not only mesmerized by their images on TV but read about them in supermarket tabloids and see them in omnipresent cosmetic ads.

Few women or men seek the overwhelming attention claimed by supermodels, but huge numbers of ordinary Americans are caught up in their own attention performances oriented around fashion and beauty. Millions of women—including teenagers who spend hours gazing dreamily at the supermodels—vie for attention with a near obsessive dedication to the look of their own bodies and the making of their own fashion statements. Teenage girls spend hours in front of the mirror making up their hair and faces, dressing themselves, and practicing their own version of a walk down the runway—in this case the mall or the school corridor—with their audience being not only boys but other girls whom they seek to impress.[2]

Grooming for attention is hardly a new phenomenon but it assumes an increasingly frantic and commodified form in today's culture. Fashion displays have become pathologically central to identity, as manifested by the spread of serious eating disorders, which prove the urgency that young women and many men attach to physical attention. Thousands are literally starving themselves and millions are compulsively dieting to make themselves worthy of it.[3]

The rapidly growing popularity among adults of facial plastic surgery, thigh tucking, celluloid removal, bone shaving, and other forms of cosmetic surgery, as well as pervasive dieting, suggests that the pursuit of attention through physical display has become a lifelong enterprise. Women start young—alarmingly, parents now are known to give their teenage daughters cosmetic surgery as graduation gifts—but a growing number of men of all ages are devoted to their own body displays. They pump iron, buy steroids for muscle growth or prescriptions for new hair-growing drugs, or shop to find the sexy underwear modeled in the Calvin Klein ads or the fashionable suits marketed in *Esquire* or *George*. Even preteenage boys are reported to be anxious about the size of their muscles or the sex appeal of their hair. The horrific 1999 Columbine High School killings in Colorado, in a school celebrating supermuscular football players whose pictures lined the corridors, were partly a desperate cry for attention by scrawny outcasts whose bodies didn't measure up. Meanwhile, throngs of both boys and girls exhibit green or orange hair and pierced noses, navels, or tongues, in the multiple forms of body mutilation and punk fashion that are among the most brazen means of attracting attention in teen culture.[4]

The channeling of attention pursuits through physical display and fashion reflects an unprecedented commodification of the body in modern America. A creative fashion industry engorged with profits saturates the mass media, and although it is not the prime mover behind the pursuit of attention, physical or otherwise, it feeds hungers that have deeper social roots. The supermodels' long and lean bodies and perfectly groomed faces—seducing consumers from magazine covers and TV screens everywhere—have become the impossible standard by which many ordinary teenagers and adults now measure themselves. For those most passionately involved, social interaction degrades into a competitive struggle to purvey an attention-grabbing image of beauty and sophistication.

A second, related but distinct cultural trend is the rise of intimate self-exposure as a fashionable artistic and media genre—and as a more legitimate attention-commanding subject of everyday conversation. Confessional novels have become all the rage. Our best-selling authors now include Wally Lamb, whose quasi-autobiographical fiction has made his troubled childhood a national institution, and Caroline Knapp, author of *Drinking: A Love Story*, who turned her alcoholism into a cause célèbre. Such authors, lionized by Oprah's Book Club, often have powerful messages, but they licentiously pour out family secrets and bare their souls to gain a mass audience.[5]

This pursuit of public attention through private exposure is "trickling down," nowhere more dramatically than in the rise of "trash talk" shows ranging from Jerry Springer to Jenny Jones. Such shows feature people eager to reveal everything about their dysfunctional families, childhoods, marriages, affairs, divorces, and sexual traumas. A cross between the Roman circus and the Roman forum, the shows are a potent example of the democratization of celebrity, where ordinary people can garner huge attention for their mistakes, crimes, traumas, and tragedies. The lure of attention is so powerful that people sometimes stage bizarre affairs or commit crimes simply to get themselves invited on the show. Meanwhile, fabulous profits help drive the talk shows and institutionalize the celebrity of both the talk show hosts and their attention-hungry guests.[6]

Most people never appear on talk shows, but many practice a kindred pursuit in their own social lives, seeking attention from friends or workmates by talking endlessly about their own intimate problems. Whether it be lingering traumas from a difficult childhood, current marital troubles, or simply neurotic obsessions that plague one's daily state of mind, such topics have become the stuff of ordinary conversation and a powerful means of turning attention to oneself in everyday life. In the past, such personal exposure would be considered unseemly or even sinful. In what Philip Rieff has called our new "therapeutic culture," ordinary conversation often mutates into uninhibited outpourings of personal problems and becomes a plea or contest for support. The winners entrap their listeners who, whether motivated by compassion, curiosity, or simply the rules of civility, find it difficult not to cede attention to self-revealing others with such powerful and sometimes fascinating emotional claims on it.

This points to a third crucial and profound development: the rise and entrenchment of the culture of narcissism, first documented by Christopher Lasch in his book of that name. In the 1990s, a "me, me, me" ethos was glamorized in the Seinfeld show, America's favorite sitcom featuring some of the most narcissistic characters seen on television. Narcissus, the Greek mythical model for the Seinfeld personality, died by being so smitten with the beauty of his reflection in a lake that he drowned. The Seinfeld characters, with whom the mass audience obviously identified, were so comically absorbed with talking about and promoting themselves that they could not form meaningful relationships. Conversational narcissism, which I first wrote about in this book, is the trademark of the Seinfeld crowd, and has become a subject of research by linguists, social psychologists, and anthropologists.[7]

The narcissistic personality, or what I have called the self-oriented character, is now entrenched as one of the compelling national character types in America. Such people reveal themselves through subtle but obsessional patterns of calling attention to themselves, and I imagine that every reader can immediately summon up at least one aggravating friend, colleague, or acquaintance who fits the description.

A generation ago David Riesman, in his best-selling book *The Lonely Crowd*, contrasted the traditional American inner-directed person, whose self was firmly organized around strongly held values, with the emerging other-oriented person, who had no inner core and was obsessed with winning the approval of others. Our dominant national character today seems to be a variant of the other-directed type, constantly marketing himself or herself to garner attention for a wide variety of ends. This is closely linked to needs for approval, respect, and acceptance, but suggests the stirring of an even more primitive hunger to simply be seen or recognized, as well as a self-absorption that permits little attention to others. I shall argue in the new concluding chapter that our new era is breeding isolation and insecurity that evokes among a swath of the population a consuming self-preoccupation tearing at the fabric of civil society.[8]

A fourth and unanticipated trend is the harnessing of new electronic technology to pioneer previously unimaginable ways of pursuing attention. The Internet has many democratizing possibilities, but its use as a vehicle to grab attention and its potential for fueling narcissism in millions of Americans deserves special comment. I first recognized the possibilities when I read about a young woman who had set up video cameras pointing into every room in her apartment, including her bathroom and bedroom. By beaming continuous images of her private life onto her Web site, she attracted hundreds of thousands of avid viewers, partly drawn by the fact that she sometimes walked around naked.

WebDorm is a new Web site that features a running film of the private lives of college students, who put video cameras in their dorms (though usually not pointed at their beds or into their bathrooms). The entrepreneur who founded the site reports a hurricane of applications from students: "It's become a celebrity symbol." One WebDormer at Trinity College says "All my friends want to come over and sit in front of the camera . . . They think being on the Web is like being on TV." Another Web-Dormer just brags: "So I'm on camera. Go me." Though raw or perverse exhibitionism may characterize the girl who goes naked on camera for a Web audience, it is not the driving force behind the pursuit of attention today. At work among the students is a pedestrian but deep need for recognition, acceptance, respect, and—among more than a few WebDormers—a hunger for celebrity-like prestige, glamor, and importance. Noticing that WebDorm is making stars out of their students, professors have e-mailed the site proposing a "ProfessorCam." The Internet pursuit of attention is for everyone.[9]

The explosion of home movies on TV, broadcast on shows such as "America's Funniest Home Videos" and MTV's "Real World," marked an early step in the new electronic pursuit of attention. The huge popularity of these shows, especially among youths, has opened up other digital venues for mass attention available to nearly everyone. Home video displays are now standard fare on the Internet.

A growing crowd of elites and plain folk have found endless ways to exploit the Internet for attention. I first heard some years ago about a faculty member who had created a web site with a counter on it (now a standard feature) so that he could check each day the number of people who had hit on his site. Of course, the very act of constructing a personal web site can be a means to win attention, and thousands of people are building them to entice friends and strangers to look at their pictures, read about their accomplishments, and mull over their poems, diaries, or descriptions of themselves. It is now easy to make the web sites interactive, so the electronic audience can send in fan mail.

Businesses have learned how to exploit this hunger for attention on the Internet and TV. Many corporations routinely advertise their products with footage of enthusiastic consumers or clients who will say anything to get on television. Amazon.com caters to its authors' narcissism by putting forward one of the most closely watched numbers on the Internet among writers: the sales ranking of their books. More than a few writers check the number daily; likewise, people can now type in their name on the search engines at Alta Vista or Excite to find out what kind of attention the world is giving them.

Many other new technologies have become handy tools in the race for attention. Cell phones allow attention-hungry individuals to receive calls anywhere, anytime and check how many people are clamoring to get a hold of them. Getting constant calls may be intrusive, but it is a novel way of getting attention and reassuring self and others of one's importance.

Attention hunger has begun to reshape our economy and politics. Money has hardly faded from importance, and naked profit unambiguously drives our economic order more explosively than ever. But the motives that animate people within the system, particularly ambitious types bent on rising to the top, seem increasingly to be not only getting rich but also winning the kind of attention that assures them that they are important and worthy.

One index of this is the sheer frenzy with which the cream of the crop—or those bent on becoming seen as such—pursue attention via the media. Regarding one ambitious young journalist on the make, a TV producer told a reporter: "As long as you're writing about him, he doesn't care what you say." Lawyers such as Alan Dershowitz or Jonathan Turley exemplify professionals who parlay their skills to maintain an eternal life in the media; Dershowitz pops up on nearly every network talk show in Washington and New York, and Turley in 1998 managed to appear ten successive weeks on the Sunday talk shows, prompting one show reportedly to call itself a "Turley-free zone." Lawyer William Ginsburg, once Monica Lewinsky's attorney, managed a grand slam of appearances on all five top Sunday talk shows on one day, leading a pundit to say that everyone now is "trying for the Ginsburg award."[10]

Success at the pinnacle of business is being redefined in terms of achieving Madonna-style celebrity as well as Gates-style wealth. The wealthy of earlier eras tended to covet seclusion; last century's robber barons built their fabulous Newport summer mansions partly to command public attention, but they zealously guarded their personal privacy. Today, the wealthy and successful crowd seem far more ready and often embarrassingly eager to embrace the attention that the celebrity-hungry media shower upon them. Donald Trump has become a model of the self-promoting CEO. Formerly known for their reclusiveness, executives now make frequent appearances on TV shows such as the Fox News Network's Cavuto Business Report and relish the spotlight, often deferring to hosts, who make a tiny fraction of their guests' salaries, in the hopes of being invited back. When Honeywell acquired Allied Signal in 1999, Honeywell's CEO, Michael Bonsignore, said: "Maybe one day I'll have my grandchild make a scrapbook of all the stuff. I worked hard to develop credibility at Honeywell and being in the spotlight feels like the next logical step, and one that I'm enjoying very much."[11]

Few professionals and hardly any nonprofessional blue- or white-collar workers will identify with the Dershowitz or Trump version of the pursuit, but whether they admire or hate such celebrities, many are finding their own ways to pursue attention at their jobs. Think only of your work team or department meetings and the kinds of competition for air time that may go on.

Are there not a few workmates or colleagues who constantly hog the floor? Such people create a competitive dynamic in which other people find it hard to listen and may end up imitating them if only to get heard. Then the others join the pursuit, fidgeting and barely listening until they can get their own air time.

The most common forms of the pursuit are these more pedestrian interpersonal gambits, which are usually so subtle or routine that people do not recognize them unless somebody complains about them. Nonetheless, the mundane attention-hoggers have a powerful impact on ordinary interactions, initiating through their monopolization of conversation a form of "micro-aggression" that can silence others and make it difficult for anyone to listen to anyone else. This not only distresses individuals but overlays the already fiercely competitive workplace with a new pattern of interpersonal stress that can undermine both efficiency and community at work.

For a great many ordinary Americans, conspicuous consumption is the preferred form of the pursuit. Consuming is the great American pastime, as I note in Chapter 4, but in recent years the stakes have been raised in the manic consumer contest that calls attention to our own success, sexuality, or refined tastes. Many of us max out credit cards to buy expensive cars that tell everyone on the street what a success we are. We now spend tens of thousands of dollars on weddings, bar-mitzvahs, and other family ceremonies to broadcast our wealth or status. We buy pricey homes as our most lavish displays of self. High-priced designer clothes and jewelry are a "three-fer," calling attention to our income, sexiness, and aesthetic sensibility.[12]

Buying gifts has become a complex matter intertwined with the pursuit of attention. Our gifts not only express feelings to others but call attention to our own success or taste, and merchandisers and marketers—who sell more than one-third of their wares at Christmas—encourage this nuanced form of self-display packaged as generosity to others. Students of philanthropy note that gifts by the wealthy to universities, museums, or libraries are much more likely now than several decades ago to bear the name of the donor. So, too, our personal gifts have become subtle statements mainly about ourselves.

Conspicuous consumption in all its splendid variety is the retailer's dream. The explosion of sophisticated advertising that plays on our ego and vulnerabilities, such as ads for cosmetics that promise to make us less plain or less old, seduces millions of ordinary Americans into the consumer-based pursuit. Nearly a half century ago, Thorstein Veblen introduced the idea of conspicuous consumption as a status marker among the wealthy, but its stunning spread among ordinary people might surprise even Veblen.[13]

We also see politicians pursuing attention in novel public and private ways as we move into a new era of politics as spectacle. Politics in every age has a quality of theater, and politicians from Caesar to Napoleon have been driven by overweening egos and an insatiable hunger for public adulation. But rarely has politics turned so transparently into a race for attention as in turn-of-the-millennium America, where the passion for power seems rivaled only by the desire to be in the public eye.

The political pursuit of attention reached a sublimely absurd pinnacle during the Clinton and Lewinsky sex scandal, in which so many of the players seemed to morph into surreal publicity hounds. Congressman Bob Barr, for example, one of the Republican House impeachment managers, typified the transformation of politician into aspiring media star, grooming himself to appear regularly for months on one or another talking-head TV show. Journalist Jennifer Mendelsohn noted that Barr had a reputation of being "superhumanly available" to the press, and one beseiged TV producer noted that "He'll come on at the drop of a hat." On the other side of the aisle, Democratic Congresswoman Sheila Jackson Lee, also a leading performer in the Lewinsky drama, is reported to have hogged the podium in Congress or any other available stage for countless hours and was described by *Newsday*'s Elaine Povich as "like the Energizer bunny.

She keeps going and going and going and going." Likewise, Democratic Senator Robert Torricelli of New Jersey "is absolutely shameless," being so hungry for press that, according to the *Baltimore Sun*'s Karen Hosler, before an event "has even happened, Torricelli has already faxed out his comments on it."[14]

Presidents are the symbol of an era, and our two-term Presidents Reagan and Clinton are "great communicators" who come alive only when they are in the public eye. As an actor, Reagan had always lived in front of the camera, and while he was not a shameless publicity hound, his political identity became essentially a public performance before a camera. Reagan inaugurated a period when politics degraded into theater and politicians became pitchmen mainly skilled at charming and manipulating public attention.

Bill Clinton, though not a professional actor, came to be seen as a man who lacked an inner core and gained his identity only by being seen and embraced by the masses. Clinton could escape his black moods during his scandal-plagued second term only when he plunged into the crowd, turning the Presidency into an eternal campaign for public attention and acclaim. Clinton sucked in the adulation like an asthmatic gasping for oxygen. In such attention-driven governance, the process of policy-making degenerated into Dick Morris–type focus group politics. Clinton's was a politics largely devoid of substance but masterfully calculated to win public approval and keep the President, even when morally discredited, as a seductive figure magnetizing public attention.

When politics becomes theater and politicians celebrities, it signals a degradation of public discourse and a threat to meaningful democracy. The substance of politics fades behind show, and politicians who lack serious ideas act mainly to stay high in the polls, entertain the masses, and win attention. The views of celebrities with no special competence on issues, such as Michael Jordan, Ted Turner, or Roseanne Barr, get media attention in political debate, and, given the superficiality of political life, these players seem increasingly indistinguishable from the politicians themselves.

For ordinary Americans this can be profoundly disenchanting, encouraging apathy, cynicism, and "cocooning," or a retreat into private life. When people tune in to politics at all, it is increasingly to watch political sitcoms such as the Lewinsky scandal. And for those who want to enter local politics, or for young people with a nascent interest in civic issues or social justice, the national models can easily corrupt. Many high school and college students volunteer for service projects or engage in extracurricular activities mainly to win the attention of admissions officers or corporate recruiters who emphasize the importance of well-rounded personalities.

The pursuit of attention arises in all cultures in all periods of history because attention is a fundamental human need and its exchange is a generally pleasurable necessity of social life. Getting attention satisfies basic needs ranging from respect to self-esteem to simply the sense of being present and belonging; it is hardly surprising that people everywhere desire attention to one degree or another and that all cultures make it possible for people to get it. If it seems that I have already grouped together a variety of behaviors and people under the attention rubric, it is because attention is one of the great generic currencies of social life. Like money, it can be used for many different psychological or social goals and can be exchanged for gain or fun in nearly all human interaction. Nonetheless, for the same reasons that it is sensible for economists to analyze money as a distinct phenomenon despite the huge array of different uses to which it is put, so social analysts need to understand attention as a singular phenomenon, recognizing that many different human motives underlie its pursuit and that the most avid pursuers may differ from each other in important ways.

What distinguishes one society or one era from another are the intensity of the hunger for attention, the ways people compete or cooperate to satisfy it, and how mutualistic and egalitarian the ultimate distribution of attention becomes. I argued originally that the United States was breeding a self-preoccupied citizenry and leadership class marked by a highly individualistic and competitive pursuit of attention. I propose now that we see signs of a deepening and widening of the pursuit, with particularly disturbing forms among economic and political elites, reflecting disintegrative social forces and raising serious questions about the possibilities of sustaining community.

As noted earlier, I cannot prove the historical argument that the American dynamic has worsened, nor the comparative argument that the problem is more troublesome here than in other societies. I suspect that many societies share aspects of the problems discussed here, and, as noted earlier, there remain in the United States many individuals, families, and communities who are not avid participants in the pursuit. I rely on illustration and evidence now available to explore the nature and extent of the problem, and will follow with the skeptical reader the results of current historical and comparative research studies by other scholars of conversational narcissism and related topics before making any final assessment. In the Conclusion I will review the disturbing social forces that I believe magnify the pursuit of attention today into a disruptive crisis of civil society, but I will also discuss the more hopeful developments and possibilities that can produce a more humane and generous social life.

Even if the present pursuit in America is mirrored in other nations or in earlier periods of history, that possibility offers little reason for complacency. The current problem reflects and generates too much personal pain and social devastation to be ignored. For whenever the pursuit of attention turns into a national obsession, there lurks the danger of a breakdown of social life based on the emotional unavailability of each of us to one another. An age of self-absorption is not friendly to either democracy or community, and a heightened competition for attention in ordinary conversation or other areas of everyday life suggests we could be hanging on the edge of a cliff that drops into less subtle forms of social ungluing. But we are far from doomed to fall to such depths and, as I discuss in the Conclusion, can change what we have helped create.

We turn first to a closer examination of the pursuit. In the Introduction to the first edition, I explain why the book is divided into two parts and how I collected the conversations and case studies that serve as evidence for my argument. After Part I, which uses a zoom lens to focus on how people pursue attention in ordinary conversation, I explain in the Introduction to Part II why we need also to take a wide-angle lens on the problem. Part II dissects the economic and social structures that shape how men and women and people of higher and lower classes engage in different versions of the pursuit and come away with different rewards. It also explains why so many of us—whatever our gender, class, or race—seem so dedicated to the chase.

Part IInformal Dynamics*Individualism*

"I was saying," continued the Rocket, "I was saying——what was I saying?"

"You were talking about yourself," replied the Roman Candle.

"Of course; I knew I was discussing some interesting subject when I was so rudely interrupted. . . ."

OSCAR WILDE, from "The Remarkable Rocket"

Introduction

Without attention being exchanged and distributed, there is no social life. A unique social resource, attention is created anew in each encounter and allocated in ways deeply affecting human interactions.

The quality of any interaction depends on the tendencies of those involved to seek and share attention. Competition develops when people seek to focus attention mainly on themselves; cooperation occurs when the participants are willing and able to give it. In cooperative interactions attention is distributed to each person according to his or her needs, while in competitive interactions attention is typically dominated by those most powerful. In extreme instances, certain people monopolize attention while others do not receive even the minimum allowing them to feel included or visible.

This book explores the dynamics of attention found in American society. I have distinguished between "formal" behavior, dictated by institutionally defined status and roles, and "informal" behavior, activity not formally prescribed. In Part I, I consider the informal behavior that emerges when people have some freedom from their formal obligations, primarily in conversations with friends and acquaintances in everyday life. In studying everyday conversation, I have found a pervasive tendency for individuals to seek predominant attention for themselves. I shall suggest that this pattern is rooted in an American cultural individualism which encourages self-interest and self-absorption.

Even in informal conversations, where people do not have strictly defined roles, they are not entirely free to disregard formal status requirements.[1] Pure "informal" behavior thus does not occur in any setting and is discussed in Part I as a model never fully realized in social life. In Part II, when I turn to "formal" behavior that occurs in both institutionally regulated interactions and in informal conversations, I explore the limits of this initial model.

In Part II, I focus on the relation between attention and status. This relation is most pronounced in the formal interactions at workplaces and other institutional settings where attention is channeled to those in authority. In all interactions, the amount of attention any individual receives is shaped by gender, social class, and other factors that determine one's worth. The dynamics of attention in America are intricately meshed with the stratification system of the society as a whole, and I shall show that inequalities in the distribution of attention are linked to broader social inequality.

The relation between the dynamics of face-to-face interaction and the larger society underlies my approach here. My focus on social interaction falls within the domain of what has traditionally been called "micro" sociology. Growing out of Georg Simmel's work on the sociology of interpersonal life and Erving Goffman's work on face-to-face relations, microsociology has been kept largely separate from "macro" sociology, which is the analysis of economic, political, social, and cultural systems. Theorists of the "micro" have typically "bracketed" or ignored the larger institutional theater where interpersonal dynamics are played. Conversely, the great traditions of "macro" sociology, including Marxism and other paradigms of historical and socioeconomic analysis, have lacked a close treatment of face-to-face interaction.

Some social theorists, however, have attempted to integrate these perspectives. C. Wright Mills and Hans Gerth, in a work receiving insufficient consideration today, developed a model for social psychology linking face-to-face dynamics and institutional systems in which "the structural and historical features of modern society [are] connected with the most intimate features of man's self."[2] A related framework was introduced by Erich Fromm, who argued for the development of a "dynamic" social psychology where the principal forms of interpersonal behavior, social character, and consciousness would be analyzed in relation to the dominant socioeconomic system. In a discussion that has influenced my own perspective, Fromm argued that individualism is a key factor in the organization of social relations in modern Western societies, suggesting that the norms of egoism, self-interest, and competition that prevail in the capitalist marketplace significantly affect interactions and character in the United States and other contemporary Western societies.[3]

In this book I explore dynamics of everyday face-to-face behavior within the context of the culture and socioeconomic system of American society. My focus in Part I is on the individualistic attention-behavior found especially in informal social life. By individualistic behavior, I mean self-interested, egoistic action displaying lack of concern and responsibility for others. In social interaction, one form this takes is seeking to monopolize attention. It occurs primarily in informal conversations where people are freed from institutionally defined tasks and obligations and are at liberty to focus on themselves.

In the first chapter I show that American cultural norms encourage a subtle attention to oneself, as everyone is expected to assume responsibility for his own needs and is required to take only minimal initiative to assure others' attention. Informal attention-behavior mirrors broader forms of American individualism which establish individual initiative and self-concern as primary virtues. In the second chapter I explore a set of pervasive attention-practices reflecting a psychology of self-absorption and narcissism. These all involve ways that American conversationalists act to turn the topics of ordinary conversations to themselves without showing sustained interest in others' topics. Such "conversational narcissism" is explored as the main expression of an individualistic psychology that turns much of social life in America into the pursuit of self-gratification.

Extremely individualistic societies are vulnerable to a disintegration of social life in which needs and desires for egoistic gratification overwhelm the social order. In America, the individualistic psychology underlying conversational narcissism is one of broad self-absorption, bred by cultural and economic individualism and the emergence of the "self" cut adrift from any enduring community. While I focus in Part I on the specific dynamics of conversation, I explore in the final chapter the societal conditions that encourage, indeed, require, such "self-orientation."

When we consider the formal interactions that take place in schools, workplaces, and other institutions, it becomes clear that attention and status are closely linked. In the informal interactions considered in Part I, differences of status and role are less emphasized than in highly structured institutional settings. In formal interactions, the right to pursue attention for oneself and to receive it from others is conditioned by one's institutional roles and social power. I thus turn in the second part of the book to what I call the "formal" dynamics of attention, concerned with the ways that status and official power dictate attention-behavior and shape the amount of attention that people receive.

formal
status
power
role

This requires going beyond the work of Goffman and others who have explored status and deference in interpersonal life toward an analysis of the ways that face-to-face relations are uniquely embedded within the dominant socioeconomic system—in this instance, within the patriarchal system and class structure of contemporary America. I have indicated that microsociologists have neglected analysis of the larger economic and political institutions. Face-to-face behavior always takes place, however, within a larger societal context. I show in Part II that the allocation and distribution of attention, much like the allocation and distribution of wealth, is uniquely structured by the prevailing socioeconomic system, reflecting pervasive hierarchical patterns of power and prestige.

While I remain focused on the ways that people give and get

attention, the analysis in Part II moves back and forth between the structure of face-to-face relations and features of larger institutions. I show that patriarchy and the class system lead to important differences between men and women and between dominant and subordinate economic groupings in ways of exchanging attention and prospects of receiving it. Women and members of subordinate socioeconomic groups are assigned roles that require the subordination of self and the giving of attention. Their psychology and attention-behavior thus vary from the patterns discussed in Part I and are analyzed as key face-to-face expressions of social inequality.

The analysis in this book is based on research carried out by the author examining the exchange and distribution of attention in social interactions. The original study, the "Attention-Interaction Project," involved field studies of face-to-face interactions in six designated settings: family households, workplaces, restaurants, classrooms, dormitories, and therapy groups. Trained observers, working from a standardized observation guide, studied fifteen hundred interactions in these settings, focusing on the amount of visual and topical[4] attention given each participant and factors determining who receives the most and least attention.

The observers wrote qualitative accounts of the following: (1) the differing personality and interactional styles of those at the top and bottom of the "attention-hierarchy," (2) the effect of gender and social status on the ability of each participant to gain and hold attention, (3) the kinds of competition for attention and the ways in which they were resolved, (4) the relation between the institutional roles and power of each participant and the attention he or she received, (5) the relative equality or inequality in the distribution of attention, (6) factors creating extreme inequality, and (7) the relative disposition of each participant to seek attention for himself or herself. Carried out in natural settings, these observations provide rich source material about attention in a wide variety of ordinary interactions. I have drawn extensively on them as preliminary evidence and illustrative data for the hypotheses and ideas advanced throughout the book.[5]

The second project involved the tape-recording and transcription of one hundred informal dinner conversations among acquaintances and friends in restaurants, dining halls, and households. Each conversation involved the participation of different volunteers; altogether, the study involved the participation of 320 conversationalists.[6]

These transcripts permitted a more precise analysis of the exchange and distribution of attention in conversation. Special consideration was given to whose topics were discussed and the specific processes by which people seek to turn the conversation to themselves. These transcripts provided extensive and detailed raw conversational data for interpreting individualistic attention-behavior.

This study is an exploratory effort to develop methods of social analysis and derive conclusions concerning the relation of face-to-face processes to larger institutions. The analysis of attention offers a methodology for exploring the psychology and social relations bred by individualism and the nature of power and status in everyday life. Such an investigation can hopefully point to a comprehensive social theory illuminating everyday life in America as an expression of its dominant cultural traditions and political economy.

1 Every Man for Himself; Every Woman for Herself Individualism Face-to-Face

Each individual is conscious of himself, but nobody is conscious of themselves collectively. . . .

THOMAS HARDY, from *The Woodlanders*

Psychologists have treated attention as a fundamental human need. John Bowlby and René Spitz, for example, while studying the emotional development of infants, concluded that the baby's need for attention is similar to that for food.[1] Infants who receive less than a required minimum of attention may die or develop grotesque physical and emotional aberrations.

R. D. Laing, in early studies of adult psychiatric patients, found a common preoccupation with being seen or simply being noticed.[2] He showed that emotional deterioration frequently results from a form of attention-starvation and that psychotic symptoms can in many cases be pinpointed as obsessive attention fantasies. The paranoid person who feels that everyone is looking at or talking about him may simply be creating in his imagination the attention lacking in his everyday life. The "Napoleonic Complex" and other delusions of grandeur are extreme ways to overcome the feeling of never being noticed.

What distinguishes Laing's patients is not the need for attention but a disadvantage in claiming the amount or kind that permits others to maintain sanity. Most people have desires or needs for attention which they seek to satisfy in everyday life. People differ mainly in their success in gratifying their needs.

In this book I am not concerned with attention as a psychological need per se, but rather with the social conditions that affect how much attention people seek to gain and determine how much different people receive.[3] The rules governing the exchange of attention are a basic feature of each society's culture and as such reveal much about its fundamental assumptions. Who gets attention—in individual face-to-face encounters and in institutional arenas like the family or the workplace—is closely linked to social power and illuminates the status hierarchy of society.

ATTENTION AND THE STRUCTURE OF FACE-TO-FACE INTERACTION

Attention is given and received in all interactions, whether it be lovemaking, informal conversation, or encounters at work. While people can be the object of attention outside the context of face-to-face interaction—on television, over the phone, or as the object of another's thinking—I am concerned here only with face-to-face attention. I shall concentrate especially on a form to be called "focused" or "commonly focused" attention.

Commonly focused attention is the kind exchanged in "focused" interaction, defined by Erving Goffman as ". . . the kind of interaction that occurs when people gather close together and openly cooperate to sustain a single focus of attention, typically by taking turns at talking."[4] Focused interactions are mainly conversations—both informal and those regulated by institutionally defined roles. These can be distinguished from "unfocused" interactions where people simply pass in and out of each other's view.[5] The unique feature of focused interaction is the development of a common focus of attention. There are both a visual and a cognitive common focus of attention in conversation. The visual focus is the person being looked at, normally the person speaking. The cognitive focus is the person being talked about, the person or object who is the topic or "subject" of the conversation.[6]

The question of who should be the focus—and how much visual and cognitive attention each person should receive—arises in every social interaction. Thus, as with economic resources, there is a problem of allocating and distributing attention. Accordingly, one can ask the following kinds of questions: How much equality exists in the amount of attention given to different participants? Are there interactional classes of "rich" and "poor" corresponding to those who typically receive large and small shares of attention? Is attention allocated on a cooperative or competitive basis? Every society evolves a set of rules for organizing and allocating attention which reflects a particular way of answering these questions.

Different attention dynamics develop in informal and formal interactions. Informal interactions are those in which people do not have institutionally defined roles or tasks to perform. These include all the ordinary conversations that take place among friends and acquaintances in everyday life. Formal interactions are ones tightly structured by institutionally defined roles and tasks, such as interactions in the classroom or doctor's office. In these interactions, who gets attention is determined differently than in informal interactions, largely by the organization and requirements of the roles themselves.[7]

INFORMAL INTERACTION
AND INDIVIDUAL INITIATIVE

The informal attention-behavior that occurs in everyday conversations in America is individualistic and mirrors broader forms of individualism in American life. In an individualistic culture, each person must assume responsibility primarily for himself or herself.[8] In America, the dominant culture of individualism has traditionally emphasized competition and individual initiative as principles of social conduct.[9] Allocation of attention is associated with special forms of individual responsibility and competition.

Who gets attention in informal conversation is determined primarily by competing individual initiatives. Each individual is responsible for himself, with his share of attention determined largely by his own efforts and skills. Each is relatively free, within the limits of civility, to take as much initiative as desired and to command as much of the attention as he can.[10]

The term "initiative" is used here to mean any active assertion to gain or keep attention. Efforts to attract attention can be called *gaining initiatives* and include moves to gain the floor or to introduce one's own topics. Efforts to hold the attention once it is gotten, either by continuing to speak or prolonging one's topics can be called *sustaining initiatives*. How much attention anyone receives is decided primarily by the frequency and persistence of both types of initiatives and their success in competition with others.[11]

People vary in aggressiveness and style because of differences in personality, gender, and social status. Certain individuals seek the floor more boldly than others and introduce their own topics more forcefully. Some people are more animated, dramatic, or expressive, traits which contribute to success in both winning the floor and holding it. Furthermore, as the content of what is said clearly affects how others respond, intelligence, humor, and sensitivity all bear on the effectiveness of gaining and sustaining initiatives.

INDIVIDUALISM AND COMPETITION

In America, informal attention-behavior is individualistic in the sense that each person takes initiative for his or her share without assuming responsibility for others. As long as they observe the norms of civility, people are free to concentrate on the gratification of their own needs.[12] We can understand this more precisely by distinguishing between *attention-getting* initiatives (the gaining- and sustaining-initiatives already discussed) and *attention-giving* initiatives. Attention-giving initiatives are designed to steer attention to others and include active efforts to introduce topics about them or to support their subjects already set forth. Except under special circumstances, as when someone expresses pain or great distress, conversationalists are not required to make any attention-giving initiatives. This is reflected in the tendency to initiate topics about oneself far more often than about others, as shown clearly in the dinner conversation interpreted below.

With one exception, each topic about one of the participants is initiated by that person himself or herself. In my analysis of one hundred dinner conversations this pattern is the characteristic one.[13] People concentrate on initiating topics about themselves and assume that others will do the same.[14]

This does not mean, however, that conversationalists are not under any obligation to give attention. People are expected to indicate that they are listening while others are speaking, either by looking at them and nodding or by making acknowledgments such as "mmm" or "uh huh."[15] In addition, there are even certain obligations of polite initiative-taking to assure others of minimal attention. One is the mandatory ritual at the onset of conversations to express interest in others through inquiries such as "How are you?" Such expressions maintain civility and assure each conversationalist a ritual quotient of attention that I call "civil attention." This includes initial eye contact that indicates inclusion as a participant as well as greetings. It entails over the full course of a conversation the right to complete a sentence or brief thought, to get eye contact from others while speaking, and to expect that other speakers will not blatantly ignore one's interests, ideas, or reactions.

Everyone is in a competitive position in a conversation because the amount of attention received depends on the relative success of one's own initiatives to attract and hold the common

Topic Number	Topic Subject	Topic-Initiator
1.	Dan's plans for the evening	Dan
2.	Food	Jim
3.	Dinner schedule	Kay
4.	Kay's art work	Jim
5.	Food	Dan
6.	Kay's job	Kay
7.	Jim's job	Jim
8.	Dan's lunch	Dan
9.	Dan's afternoon conversation	Dan
10.	Food	Kay

focus.[16] Commonly focused attention within any interaction is limited and can become "scarce" if the amount any person seeks is greater than that available.[17] Under conditions of unusual scarcity, the competitive features become more visible and pronounced. The participants—in large groups, for example—may openly vie with one another to gain the floor by interrupting or shouting one another down. However, in most settings the competition remains disguised because they are expected to be more subtle and discreet.

THE PROBLEM OF INVISIBILITY

There is a striking parallel between the individualistic and competitive processes of attention-getting and certain forms of economic behavior. In a classic capitalist economic model rewards are allocated through competitive individual initiative with no limits placed on what share of the total rewards (within a given market) any individual (or firm) can gain. This leads to inequalities determined by relative competitive power rather than needs. Similarly, in informal interactions there is no assurance that each individual will get the attention he wants because competitive individual initiative again decides allocation, with no limits on how much (or how little) anyone should receive. Certain people can dominate or monopolize the attention while others may be unsuccessful in claiming even the minimal share required to feel included.

Poverty has an interactional parallel in "invisibility," where one or more listeners can gain hardly any attention. It occurs when the norms of face-to-face behavior offer insufficient protection against being ignored or overlooked. The "invisible" person does not gain even the minimum attention required to feel that his or her presence has been acknowledged and established.

In America the norms governing informal conversation do not require anyone to give attention to persons who, for reasons of personality or social status, are unable to command it through their own initiatives. While each conversationalist is assured a minimal amount of civil attention, some people experience difficulty in making themselves visible in ordinary talk. For example:

Five people are sitting eating lunch. They are engaged in a lively conversation about changes in marriage. Four of the five take an active role, breaking in frequently with comments about themselves and their experiences in relationships. The fifth member, Bill, who is less forceful and self-assured than the others, has trouble gaining the floor. He makes several efforts to speak, but someone louder or more persistent interrupts each time and he gives way. The third or fourth time this happens, he becomes very agitated and abruptly turns to the woman next to him to initiate a side conversation. He begins to tell her what he wanted to say to the group. She gives him eye contact and listens for about a minute, but then her attention is captured by what someone in the main discussion is saying and so, touching his arm briefly, turns back to the others. He also turns his attention back to the main conversation, but makes no further efforts to speak and does not get any attention from the others.[18]

A variety of personality traits can render an individual vulnerable to this kind of invisibility. Being less assertive, aggressive, or animated, or especially shy or insecure often leads to difficulties in getting attention.[19] In the illustration above, lack of forcefulness and self-assurance became a major handicap in what was a spirited competition for the floor. Bill was extended no help or support through openings from the others and was forced to rely on his own initiatives. The attempt to initiate a side conversation, his way of seeking to win at least some marginal attention, succeeded only briefly in relieving his invisibility in the main conversation.

Observations of informal conversations in restaurants and living rooms suggest that an unequal distribution of attention typically develops. As the number of people increases, it is more likely that one or more will get little or no attention, this being reported frequently in conversations involving more than two people.[20] Invisibility is thus a common experience, although usually unseen by those free of it, as there are no routine means by which invisible participants can call attention to their state.[21]

In conversations between two people attention is less scarce and problems of invisibility less intractable. Nonetheless, one of the conversationalists can fade into invisibility if the other monopolizes the talking time or keeps the topic always focused on himself or herself. There are ritual prohibitions against such behavior reflected in apologies when blatantly violated. Common ones are "Oh, I see I've done nothing but talk about myself," or "Gee, I hope I haven't bored you with all these personal problems." If there is still time, the offender may extend an opening to the other; "Well, enough about myself. What have you been up to?" or "Now I want to hear all about you." However, because these offerings frequently are made near the end of conversation, they may serve to make ritual amends without significantly increasing reciprocity. Moreover, the offender often remains completely unaware of the other's invisibility and even the victim, as long as his or her rights to civil attention have been fulfilled, may only come to realize afterward that the conversation has never stayed on his or her topics.

2 Monopolizing the Conversation On Being Civilly Egocentric

"Conversation indeed," said the Rocket. "You have talked the whole time yourself. That is not conversation."

"Somebody must listen," answered the Frog, "and I like to do all the talking myself."

"You are a very irritating person," said the Rocket, "and very ill bred. I hate people who talk about themselves, as you do, when one wants to talk about oneself, as I do. . . ."

OSCAR WILDE, from "The Remarkable Rocket"

Individualism has a counterpart in American psychology. People tend to seek attention for themselves in face-to-face interactions. This attention-getting psychology reflects an underlying character structure of "self-orientation" that emerges in highly individualistic societies.[1] Erich Fromm has theorized that a shared character structure develops in each society, a "social character" that is a response to the requirements of the social order and best suited for survival and success within it. The self-oriented character type develops a highly egocentric view of the world and is motivated primarily by self-interest. To cope with social and economic insecurity bred by individualism, he becomes preoccupied with himself. His "attention-getting" psychology is thus rooted in a broad self-absorption engendered by social conditions highly developed in contemporary America.[2]

In informal conversation, the self-oriented person repeatedly seeks to turn attention to himself. This "conversational narcissism" is closely related to the individualistic norms already discussed. As shown in the first chapter, attention is allocated according to norms in which each individual is responsible for himself, and is free, within limits of civility, to take as much as he can. These norms legitimate focusing on one's own needs in informal talk and are consistent with the effort by self-oriented conversationalists to gain predominant attention for themselves.

THE FORMS OF CONVERSATIONAL NARCISSISM

Conversational narcissism is the key manifestation of the dominant attention-getting psychology in America. It occurs in informal conversations among friends, family, and coworkers. The profusion of popular literature about listening and the etiquette of managing those who talk constantly about themselves suggests its pervasiveness in everyday life; its contemporary importance is indicated by the early appearance of these problems in Emily Post's etiquette manual.[3]

In observations of ordinary conversations, I have found a set of extremely common conversational practices which show an unresponsiveness to others' topics and involve turning them into one's own.[4] Because of norms prohibiting blatantly egocentric behavior, these practices are often exquisitely subtle; ritual forms of civility and face-saving have evolved to limit the overt expression of egoism in social life.[5] Although conversationalists are free to introduce topics about themselves, they are expected to maintain an appearance of genuine interest in those about others in the conversation. A delicate face-saving system requires that people refrain from openly disregarding others' concerns and keep expressions of disinterest from becoming visible. Practices of conversational narcissism are normally, then, driven underground and expressed in disguised forms where they are not readily discerned by any member of the conversation.[6]

To explore the narcissistic practices that occur most often, we must distinguish between two kinds of attention-response: the *shift-response* and the *support-response*. The shift- and support-responses are alternative ways one can react to others' conversational initiatives. The differences between the two can be seen in the following examples:[7]

JOHN: I'm feeling really starved.
MARY: Oh, I just ate. (shift-response)
JOHN: I'm feeling really starved.
MARY: When was the last time you ate? (support-response)

JOHN: God, I'm feeling so angry at Bob.
MARY: Yeah, I've been feeling the same way toward him. (shift-response)
JOHN: God, I'm feeling so angry at Bob.
MARY: Why, what's been going on between the two of you? (support-response)

JOHN: My mother would pack me melted cheese sandwiches every day.
MARY: My mom never made me a lunch I could stand to eat. (shift-response)
JOHN: My mother would pack me melted cheese sandwiches every day.
MARY: Hey, your mother was all right. (support-response)

JOHN: I saw Jane today on the street.
MARY: I haven't seen her in a week. (shift-response)
JOHN: I saw Jane today on the street.
MARY: Oh, how's she doing? (support-response)

JOHN: I just love Brahms.
MARY: Chopin's my favorite. (shift-response)

JOHN: I just love Brahms.
MARY: Which is your favorite piece? (support-response)

The shift-response and support-response are both commonly used. They are superficially so little different that few conversationalists notice the distinction. Yet they affect the flow of attention and the development of topics in markedly different ways. When Mary uses the shift-response, she temporarily shifts the attention to herself and creates the potential for a change in topic. When using the support-response, she keeps the attention and topic securely focused on John.

Of the two responses, only the shift-response changes who is the subject of the conversation. For example, if Mary says to John, "I'm going to the movies tonight," John can temporarily make himself the subject with any of the following replies:

That reminds me, I've got to go home tonight.
I'm sick of movies these days.
Gee, I wonder what I'm going to do tonight.

With each of these shift-responses, John introduces the dilemma of whether the conversation will continue with Mary as the subject or will turn to him. Alternatively, he could offer the following kinds of support responses:

What movie?
Great, you deserve a break.
Are you feeling good enough to go?

These support-responses are attention-giving ones not in competition with Mary's initial assertion. They keep the conversation clearly focused on her and give her license to continue as the subject. Support-responses, unlike shift-responses, cannot normally be introduced to transfer attention to the self.[8]

Conversational narcissism involves preferential use of the shift-response and underutilization of the support-response. We can distinguish between active and passive narcissistic practices. The active practices involve repeated use of the shift-response to subtly turn the topics of others into topics about oneself. The passive practices involve minimal use of support-responses so that others' topics are not sufficiently reinforced and so are terminated prematurely.

Active Practices

The shift-response is the one response to another's initiative through which one can introduce one's own topic. While it does not necessarily change the topic—and is frequently not so intended—it nonetheless always creates the possibility. The following dialogue illustrates how the shift-response is typically used by self-oriented conversationalists to bring attention to themselves:

MARY: My summer place has been such a blessing this year.

JOHN: I know, I sure would like a place like that, the way I've been feeling, but I've got to earn the bread first, you know?

MARY: Yeah.

JOHN: I figure that if I work enough this year and next, I'll be able to check that place out in Vermont again and maybe. . . .

Although John appears, in his first response, to have expanded on Mary's topic, he has subtly shifted the attention to himself. He has not responded directly to her feelings but has shifted the conversation to his own state of mind, his problems with money, and his desires for a summer place of his own. Rather than returning to her topic, Mary then responds with a support-response allowing John in the following turn to consolidate his earlier topical initiative.

While changing the topic, John links his response to Mary's and prefaces his own with an acknowledgment of hers. The preface is a token gesture of recognition of what the other has said. Numerous other prefaces such as "oh really," "huh," "isn't that something," "same here," and "I can't believe it" recur in conversations. They soften the transition in topic and help to protect the individual against charges of unresponsiveness. A preface acknowledges that one is paying attention to the previous statement and adds legitimacy to an assertion in which the individual suddenly introduces himself as the subject. It also presents the interjection of oneself as not simply an effort to gain attention, but rather a form of responsiveness to share personal experience or information.[9]

Although important for maintaining civility, a shift-response does not require a preface. For example:

JOHN: I've got such a huge appetite.
BILL: I couldn't eat a thing.

JOHN: My father would take me every two weeks to a game and I spent every minute looking forward to it.
BILL: I remember the first game my father took me to. I made so much noise that he didn't want to take me anymore.

Here, the shifts in focus are legitimized by the appearance of a topical connection. The subtlety of the shift-response is that it is always based on a connection to the previous subject. This creates an opening for the respondent to shift the topic to himself while still preserving the "face" of the other.

While repeating the shift-response is the most common way self-oriented conversationalists seek attention, it does not always imply conversational narcissism. The shift-response can serve either as a sharing-response or as a narcissistic topical initiative. The major difference lies not in introducing the shift-response, but in the intent and the statements which follow. When serving narcissistic ends, shift-responses are repeated until a clear shift in subject has transpired. When meant only as sharing-responses, interjecting oneself is temporary and is quickly followed by returning to the original topic. In these instances, the shift-response only briefly brings attention to oneself as a means of furthering the conversation.

The effectiveness of the shift-response as an attention-getting device lies partly in the difficulty in distinguishing immediately whether a given response is a sharing one or a narcissistic initiative. At a certain stage in the development of another's topic, it becomes appropriate to introduce information about oneself, but normally not until the other has introduced most of his information or narrative. The earlier the initial shift-response, the more likely it foreshadows an effort to seize the conversation.[10] This is illustrated in the following conversation:

MARY: I saw the most beautiful rainbow today.
JOHN: Wow, I saw a lovely one just last week.

At this point, Mary cannot know whether John actually is interested in her experience or in simply turning the talk to himself. His statement is connected to hers and may well represent an honest attempt to share his experience or to highlight hers. But it may also signal a narcissistic initiative, which would be confirmed if he persists in using the shift response.

MARY: I saw the most beautiful rainbow today.
JOHN: Wow, I saw a lovely one just last week.
MARY: It had such a magnificent blend of blues and golds.
JOHN: Huh, the one I saw was all reds and yellows.

John's repeated shift responses have now become a competing initiative that make it more difficult for Mary to sustain her own subject. A decisive topical shift occurs in the next turn as Mary, despite her option to continue with her own topic, accommodates John's initiative with a support-response:

MARY: I saw the most beautiful rainbow today.
JOHN: Wow, I saw such a lovely one last week.
MARY: It had such a magnificent blend of blues and golds.
JOHN: Huh, the one I saw was all reds and yellows.
MARY: What time of day did you see it?
JOHN: Early afternoon. I was walking near the river and. . . .

The active narcissistic practice always follows some variation of this pattern, in which repetitions of the shift-response turn the conversation to oneself. The shift-response functions as a gaining initiative[11] which introduces one's own topic. It sets the stage for a topic competition which will persist as long as each conversationalist continues to use a shift-response. The self-oriented conversationalist triumphs in this competition when his shift-response succeeds in eliciting a succession of support-responses from others, thus securing their acquiescence to his topic.

Incessant use of the shift-response is not typical because it is too baldly egoistic and disruptive. A more acceptable—and more pervasive—approach is one where a conversationalist makes temporary responsive concessions to others' topics before intervening to turn the focus back to himself. The self-oriented conversationalist mixes shift-responses with support-responses, leaving the impression that he has interest in others as well as himself.

JIM: You know, I've been wanting to get a car for so long.
BILL: Yeah. (support-response)
JIM: Maybe when I get the job this summer, I'll finally buy one. But they're so expensive.

BILL: I was just thinking about how much I spend on my car. I think over $2500 a year. You know I had to lay out over $750 for insurance. And $850 for that fender job. (shift-response)

JIM: Yeah, it's absurd. (support-response)

BILL: I'm sick of cars. I've been thinking of getting a bicycle and getting around in a healthy way. I saw a great red racer up in that bike shop on Parkhurst Ave.

JIM: I love bikes. But I'm just really feeling a need for a car now. I want to be able to drive up the coast whenever I want. (shift-response)

BILL: Uh huh . . . (support-response)

JIM: I could really get into a convertible.

BILL: Oh, you can go anywhere on a bike. I'm going to borrow John's bike and go way up north next weekend. You know, a couple of weekends ago Sue and I rented bikes and rode down toward the Cape. . . . (shift-response)

The narcissistic initiative and the ensuing topic competition is subtle here. From a casual reading of the transcript there appears to be a responsive exchange with no readily discernible egocentricity. But a more careful examination reveals the familiar narcissistic pattern. Bill responds initially to Jim's topic with a support-response that indicates acknowledgment and at least minimal interest. Most of his subsequent responses, however, are shift-responses that change the topic from Jim's desires for a new car to a discussion of his own car and then to his own interest in bicycles. Jim makes several efforts to steer the conversation back to his original concern, but Bill's attention-getting initiatives are successful. In the end, he launches into a story about his bike trip, which decisively shifts the topic to himself.

This interchange exemplifies the pattern of active conversational narcissism. One conversationalist transforms another's topic into one pertaining to himself through persistent use of the shift-response. The topic-shift is accomplished prematurely, before the first speaker has had the opportunity to complete what he regards as the full development of his subject. Yet it is accomplished without violation of the ritual obligations of responsiveness and occasions no blatant injuries of face.

Passive Practices

Passive practices constitute a more subtle expression of narcissism, characterized not by the grabbing of attention but by miserliness in the responses given to others. Such practices involve underutilization of the support responses that normally allow others to pursue their topics. The effect is to let the other's topics die through lack of encouragement, thereby opening the floor to the initiation of one's own topics.

To analyze the passive practices which recur most frequently, we must first distinguish among three different kinds of support-responses, which I call: *the background acknowledgment, the supportive assertion,* and *the supportive question. Background acknowledgments* are abbreviated responses such as "uh huh," "yeah," "oh really," and "umm." They are the weakest of the support-responses, but their use is important because they give the appearance that one is listening and wants the speaker to continue. *Supportive assertions* are complete declarative responses to the topic initiatives of others and include evaluative statements ("I think that's great"), comments ("I never would have thought of him"), and suggestions ("You must see her right away"). A supportive assertion is a stronger response than the background acknowledgment, for it not only confirms that one is listening but indicates active engagement in the topic. *Supportive questions* are queries which draw out a speaker on his topic. They are the most encouraging of all support responses and the most active way of assuring that another's topic will be sustained.[12]

Passive practices involve *minimal use* and *differential use* of these three types of support-responses so that the topics of others are prematurely concluded. Minimal use contributes to the termination of a topic by withholding or delaying support-responses. Differential use means that a weaker support-response is chosen when a stronger one could be used.

Minimal use. Conversationalists cannot refrain from making any support-responses in the course of a conversation, as this would indicate too blatant an indifference to the other's topic.[13] Minimal use entails, then, a subtle unresponsiveness, where there is compliance with ritual expressions of attentiveness, but nevertheless a relative neglect of support-responses.

The most devastating form is the avoidance of the supportive question. While not all topics depend on such questions for their perpetuation, a high percentage are carried, particularly in the early phases, by others' queries. While a topic can be aborted at any point by lack of interest, a lack of support and interest when it is first initiated most effectively kills it. One can speak of the take-off points or critical thresholds which shape the life-expectancy of the topic. If, in the first several turns of talk, the topic reaches take-off, it is far less vulnerable to derailment by minimal use. Prior to takeoff, topics die if they do not elicit either enthusiastic background acknowledgments or responsive questions which give explicit indication of support and interest. A string of supportive questions at the opening of a topic will normally guarantee a respectable life-expectancy for the topic, while the absence of any questions at this stage can be an ominous sign which signals premature termination.

Despite their importance, supportive questions are typically discretionary; under most circumstances, conversationalists are free to ask questions but are also at liberty not to. While there are certain initiatives which call for a mandatory response (if someone says, "I'm feeling so terrible," a supportive question like "What's wrong?" would normally be expected in return), most initiatives allow for far greater discretion. If John makes a topical initiative by saying, "I saw my friend Bill today," Jim can show active interest with a supportive question such as "How's he feeling?" or "How did it go?" He commits no offense, however, if he simply offers a background acknowledgment such as "hummm" or volunteers no support-response whatsoever.

Passive conversational narcissism entails neglect of supportive questions at all such discretionary points and extremely sparse use of them throughout conversation. Listening behavior takes place but is passive. There is little attempt to draw others out or assume other forms of active listening. This creates doubt in the others regarding the interest of their topics or their rights to attention while, however, providing no clear basis for complaint about either inattentiveness or narcissism.

A second very common minimal-use practice involves the underutilization or delay of background acknowledgments. Although weaker than supportive questions, background acknowledgments such as "yeah" or "uh huh" are nonetheless critical cues by which speakers gauge the degree of interest in their topics. A variety of studies suggest that background acknowledgments facilitate the unfolding of topics and that their absence or delay can easily disrupt the development of the speaker's topic.[14]

Ritual restraints preclude withholding all background acknowledgments. Every conversationalist is expected to extend such minimal support even when he has no interest whatsoever in the topic.[15] Speakers can exploit this expectation by interjecting expressions such as "you know," subtle requests for immediate affirmations that indicate the other is paying attention. This is a way that conversationalists insecure about others' attention or interest can actively solicit support.

Despite the ritual constraints, there is sufficient freedom to permit a potent form of minimal response. While this can involve avoiding the background acknowledgment, it most often assumes the form of a delay in its insertion so that the speaker does not receive the immediate reinforcement that permits smooth continuation of his line of thought.[16] Studies have shown that background acknowledgments can be placed with precision timing and are often perfectly inserted during split-second pauses of the other's speech.[17] Conversationalists who delay their responses for up to several seconds after another speaker has paused can throw him off-balance, disrupting his flow of speech and causing him to wonder whether his listeners are genuinely interested. Repetition of the delayed response creates more gaps in the rhythm, slowing the momentum of the conversation further and suggesting the need for a change in topic.[18] Such passive narcissism is rarely a conscious device to gain attention but is nonetheless a common means by which self-oriented conversationalists "underrespond" to the topics of others and thus open the floor to their own.

Differential Use: Differential use involves the offering of the weakest support-response consistent with the demands of civility.[19] By exercising his discretion to select the least encouraging support-response, the self-oriented conversationalist hastens the termination of others' topics. This is often accomplished by the use of background acknowledgments where far stronger responses, especially a supportive question, might be more appropriate:

MARY: Oh, I had the most awful headache all day. Tom was awful at work and, uh, just kept bothering me and bothering me. And Louise, too, more of the same. I'm so sick of it.
JOHN: Yeah.

In this instance, Mary has opened with a complaint calling for a stronger, more supportive response than the one offered. Typically, with such openings, a supportive question to draw out the speaker's feelings or experiences sets the stage for fully playing out the topic.[20] By substituting the minimal acknowledgment where a question could have been asked, John discourages Mary's initiative. She has the option to continue but will find it difficult to do so in the face of repeated discouragement of this form.

Different conversationalists vary in their vulnerability to such discouragement, depending on their assertiveness, security, and other personality factors affecting their need for responsiveness from others. Those most vulnerable are those dependent on the strongest support-responses, on being drawn out through supportive questioning. Differential use will effectively silence these speakers. At the other extreme, the most aggressive conversationalists will pursue their topics even when their initiatives elicit only weak background acknowledgments or none at all. The only effective narcissistic practice with such speakers is an active one, through aggressive use of the shift-response in one's own behalf.

Successfully aborting others' topics does not always ensure a turning of conversation to oneself, but, at minimum, prepares the stage for this possibility. At topic termination any speaker may seek to initiate his or her own topic. A second topic competition can then follow which may or may not reproduce the characteristics of the one just completed. In the pure narcissistic pattern, a conversationalist will act to discourage every topic and initiate continuing competition until he or she succeeds in securely establishing his or her own. In practice, few conversationalists remain unresponsive to *all* topics of others but will exercise selective discretion, reinforcing with support-responses a limited number that are of interest and discouraging the others with minimal and differential use.

Part II Formal Dynamics *Power*

In front of, and defending, the larger political-economic structure that determines our lives and defines the context of human relationships, there is a micropolitical structure that helps maintain it. The "trivia" of everyday life—using "sir" or first name, touching others, dropping the eyes, smiling, interrupting and so on—that characterize these micropolitics are commonly understood as facilitators of social intercourse, but are not recognized as defenders of the status quo—of the state, of the wealthy, of authority, of all those whose power may be challenged. Nevertheless, these minutiae find their place on a continuum of social control which extends from internalized socialization (the colonization of the mind) at the one end to sheer physical force (guns, clubs, incarceration) at the other.

NANCY HENLEY, from "Power, Sex, and Nonverbal Communication"

Introduction

In Part I we have seen that informal attention-dynamics in America are individualistic, with people tending to seek attention for themselves. There are, however, systematic differences between the sexes and among social classes that are aspects of "formal" behavior.[1] Of prime interest is the behavior of women and subordinate class members involving self-effacement and the giving of attention to others. In Part II, focusing mainly on formal rather than informal interactions, we examine sex roles and social class prescriptions which restrict "self-orientation" among lower-status groups and dictate a distribution of attention consistent with dominant social hierarchies.

In Part I we looked solely at informal interactions where people have the greatest freedom of individual initiative and are less strictly bound by the status and role requirements that govern their behavior in more structured areas. When we turn to formal interactions, as between doctor and patient, mother and infant, or employer and employee, it becomes apparent that the way people seek and give attention and the amount they are likely to receive is significantly shaped by their social roles and their status within the major institutional hierarchies. The analysis in Part II is fundamentally concerned with the link between face-to-face processes and social structure, focusing on the way that social roles define the responsibility for giving and getting attention in formal interactions (and to a lesser degree in informal conversation) according to gender and social class.

ALLOCATING ATTENTION
IN FORMAL INTERACTIONS

We must consider first the way that attention is allocated in formal interactions. In these interactions, which are organized to accomplish specific institutional purposes, individual initiative and individual responsibility are subject to the constraints of the institutional roles the individual is expected to perform. In the formal interaction within a classroom, for example, initiatives for attention are largely governed by the teacher and student roles, the teacher being required to take those initiatives necessary to teach in the institutionally approved manner and students expected to limit their own attention-getting initiatives in a manner dictated by the educational process.

The allocation system in formal interactions is thus one of "controlled" rather than "free" initiative, determined largely by the institutional roles. Such roles can be characterized as either attention-getting or attention-giving, depending on whether the actor is expected to give or get it. The teacher role is attention-getting while that of student is attention-giving; similarly, the role of the psychiatrist is attention-giving while that of his client is attention-getting. Those in attention-giving roles are expected to make primarily attention-giving rather than attention-getting initiatives and are thus restrained from the subtle egoism permitted in informal interaction.

Roles and Status: Power and the Attention-Getting Role

The social allocation of attention-getting and attention-giving roles among different groups largely determines who gets attention in formal interactions. Individuals who typically take on attention-getting institutional roles learn to expect and seek attention for themselves, while those most often assigned attention-giving roles assume a certain socially imposed invisibility. In Part II I show, first, that the allocation of these roles is a function of power, with the great majority of attention-getting roles assigned to dominant groups and attention-giving roles to subordinate ones. I suggest that social dominance is institutionalized face-to-face through an organization of roles in families, workplaces, and politics which permits those of higher status to claim attention as their due and requires lower-status individuals to seek and accept less.

Groups that are expected to assume primarily attention-giving roles in formal interactions learn a generalized psychology that discourages focus on oneself and predisposes the individual to give attention in all phases of social life. Such an "attention-giving" psychology diverges significantly from the individualistic psychology encouraged more broadly in the culture and reflects variations in social character linked to status and dominance. Patriarchal and social class roles encourage the prevailing "self-orientation" most strongly among members of empowered groups, while fostering among women and other subordinate groups an "other-orientation" based on subordination of self and interactional deference. While I have focused in Part I only on the dominant self-oriented patterns, I explore in Part II different behaviors among those lacking power—ones of self-effacement and attention-giving closely institutionally regulated in formal settings and more subtly enforced in formal conversation.

Inequality Face-to-Face: Attention and Social Structure

Part II departs significantly from Part I because of its focus on formal interactions and its concern with institutionally-defined power; attention-processes were explored in Part I with reference to culture (individualism) while ignoring social structure. Part II introduces new themes of equality in face-to-face life and the link between interpersonal dynamics and socioeconomic power.

The concern with status differences will highlight the idea that attention is a unique face-to-face resource, allocated and distributed much like economic wealth. Attention can be understood as an interactional currency subject to distributive justice or inequity. Part II develops the thesis that social inequalities conceived in traditional social analysis as economic or political inequalities are also simultaneously "inequalities of face," institutionalized in interpersonal life and in a distribution of attention mirroring the allocation of other resources.

The inequalities of face are not simply interesting derivatives of economic and social power, but an integral dimension of their very structure. Stratification systems create distinctions of social worth that are communicated, learned, and enforced in ordinary face-to-face processes. One aspect of class hierarchy is that members of subordinate classes are regarded as less worthy of attention in relations with members of dominant classes and so are subjected to subtle but systematic face-to-face deprivations. The directing of attention to those defined by their class as "better" or more important lies at the very heart of class power as played out in everyday social relations and suggests a new vehicle for investigating the meaning of class itself.

The treatment of these problems requires certain shifts in the frame of analysis developed in Part I that deserve explicit emphasis. First, as already discussed, an examination of roles is introduced to demonstrate the way that face-to-face processes are organized according to the requirements of the dominant social structure. Second, while focusing only on the internal dynamics of interaction in Part I, I also consider in Part II the *access* of different groups to interactional settings in which they can expect attention. Members of dominant groups are privileged not only because face-to-face processes are internally structured to their advantage, but also because they have access to a greater range of interactional settings in which attention can normally be expected. A simple example is the greater capacity of the affluent to "purchase" attention by entering psychotherapy. The analysis in Part II is thus broadened to consider the diverse ways in which face-to-face dynamics interact with and reflect the larger societal context.

3 The Gift of Attention-Giving On Women Imposed

"Pray, what are you laughing at?" inquired the Rocket; "I am not laughing."

"I am laughing because I am happy," replied the Cracker.

"That is a very selfish reason," said the Rocket angrily. "What right have you to be happy? You should be thinking about others. In fact, you should be thinking about me. I am always thinking about myself, and I expect everybody else to do the same. That is what is called sympathy."

OSCAR WILDE, from "The Remarkable Rocket"

"Her voice was ever soft, gentle and low; an excellent thing in women."

SHAKESPEARE, from *King Lear*

Men and women learn to pursue attention differently and expect and accept it in different amounts.[1] In all patriarchal societies, women are typically assigned the attention-giving roles and men the attention-getting ones.[2] Accordingly, attention-giving becomes defined as a "feminine" skill and responsibility, with men gaining attention as a privilege of their gender.

FEMALE ROLES: MOTHER AS PROTOTYPE

Betty Friedan, Jessie Bernard, and other students of sex roles have found that women's roles, public and private, mirror that of the mother. The mother role is the archetypical attention-giving one, in which women must give attention without expecting an equal measure in return. This is illustrated in the following account:

Julie, about age five, picked up a child's book and began to look at the pictures while Mother read *Good Housekeeping*. Julie began showing pictures to her mother. In response, mother would look up either immediately or after a short pause, carefully look at the picture, question Julie about some aspect (e.g., "That's a sandwich?") and then comment or laugh amusedly about the book. Sometimes they would talk about Julie's experience with particular animals or kinds of food that she saw in the pictures.

During this period, Mother showed interest in all of Julie's observations, giving Julie steady eye contact whenever Julie initiated these short conversations; in general, she communicated her interest in her daughter by listening and asking questions.

Julie then put down her magazine and sat down on the bench beside her mother. She leaned her head against Mother's shoulder, put her arm around her back, and cuddled close while looking at Mother's magazine. Mother responded by leaning her head against her daughter's and pointing out pictures of interest. Eventually, however, she told Julie to remove her arm because it was bothering her. Julie complied without appearing offended but remained snuggled close.

Mother and daughter remained in this position for quite awhile. During this time mother showed increasing irritation at Julie for pointing out pictures in the magazine, for leaning too heavily against her, or for showing impatience. Mother looked up at Julie less frequently in response to her comments.

When Julie asked her mother who painted the wall, mother crossly told her that no one had painted it, that it was wallpaper. However, Julie did not modify her comments and actions in response to her mother's irritability. She still smiled much of the time and cuddled close.[3]

This observation dramatizes the child-centeredness of a typical mother-child interaction and highlights how a mother must surrender the focus of attention. The daughter initiates and pursues conversation about things she notices while the mother gives attention by listening and drawing her out. At first, the mother listens intently and responds with real interest. Her growing impatience as the interaction proceeds, however, reflects the attention-imbalance. Jessie Bernard has emphasized that in America there are no clear limitations on how much attention a mother is expected to give; in general, the "good" mother should give as much as the child seems to require.[4]

We see here that a mother can, at minimum, expect some reciprocal attention. Her child looks back at her, asks questions, and volunteers feelings. In addition, a mother does occasionally become the focus of the interaction, as when her child wants to know why she is feeling bad or seems upset.[5]

Since she has power over her child, a mother can also maintain some control over when she gives or withholds attention. In many other roles, however, women have less power to assert limits on their attention-giving. As wives or workers, for example, they are often inferior in power to those they give attention and must normally defer to their demands.

As we have suggested, there is a close relation between the mother role and the other major female roles. Privileged women are assuming professional roles: doctors, lawyers, managers. But most women remain in the classic "female" occupational roles—nurse, child-care worker, secretary, social worker, domestic—in which some form of mothering is a primary interactional requirement.

The distinctive feature of these roles is the expectation of attention-giving. The roles females assume that are attention-getting—such as movie actress or fashion model—are the exception and are available normally only to women deemed extraordinarily sexually attractive. In most of her roles and formal interactions, however, a woman assumes a certain invisibility. For example, studies of office interactions show that secretaries and receptionists are typically required to give a "motherly" focus to their bosses, which includes responding to their job-related or personal problems, while going subtly unattended themselves.[6] This pattern is also found in child care, nursing, and other work roles.[7]

As described in Chapters 1 and 2, individualistic norms require people in ordinary informal interactions to assume responsibility only for themselves and permit as much focus on oneself as can be successfully established in competition with others. However, women's roles stringently restrict such self-orientation (in their formal interactions). The mother prototype demands a non-individualistic attitude which includes responsibility for others. This differs radically from the expectations placed on males in their formal interactions and, as we shall see, reflects the inferior power of women in a patriarchy.

MALE ROLES: ATTENTION
AND PATRIARCHAL POWER

Men in patriarchal societies are expected to assume relatively few attention-giving roles. While there are important variations, men in their formal interactions generally assume roles permitting them to concentrate on their own needs and to expect predominant attention in interactions with others, especially women.

The assignment of attention-getting roles to males is closely related to their societal power. Studies of small groups demonstrate a clear relation between power and attention-getting. Robert Bales and his followers at Harvard have shown that talking time and other measures of attention correlate strongly with measures of authority and leadership. "Task-leaders" of groups, who occupy authority roles like that of the traditional patriarchal father, speak far more than the other members and receive more eye contact and communication. Applying their research methods to the family, Bales and his associates have concluded that the father has tended to play the role of the "task-leader" in the American family and most often claims the attention associated with that role.[8]

The prototypical male role in Western societies has been the traditional patriarchal father. Novelistic and anecdotal accounts indicate that the classic patriarch exercised absolute control over family interaction. Oliver Wendell Holmes wryly characterized him as the "autocrat of the breakfast table." In the nineteenth century domicile, children and wife were expected to remain quiet unless questioned or otherwise directed to speak by the father or husband. Out of fear, power, and respect, the father commanded attention and focus whenever present in the family.

Despite the decline of absolute patriarchal authority and the importance of home and hearth as a site of female influence, the father's role remains one in which he can compel special forms of attention.[9] In my field studies, I found that fathers were interrupted less often when they spoke and were listened to with greater respect and patience. They also exercised greater control over the topics discussed and were more successful in gaining the focus of attention when they sought to do so. This pattern grows out of the father's institutional position, as suggested in the observation below:

The family is eating dinner. The father appears to have a very powerful position simply because of his status as "head of the family" and because he uses this status to exert veto power over what are legitimate topics of conversation and what are not. He very often silences his children when he considers their conversation to be frivolous or "not of general interest." Silencing is accomplished by short, angry statements. While he introduces subjects of conversation by making controversial and provocative statements, he never allows follow-up discussions which contradict his original statement. He virtually never contributes to or "approves of" conversations which he does not initiate.

Here, the father dominates the interaction through aggressive assertion of his intellectual authority. As "head of household" and the bearer of higher status in the larger society, his ideas and statements carry special weight.[10] His children, sensitive to differences in power, respond to his words both because of his authority in the family and his knowledge and experience in the larger world.

Conversational patterns between husbands and wives vary greatly. Observers of husband-wife interactions reported that the wife often spoke more but also gave more supportive responses and active encouragement to her husband's talk about himself, while the husband listened less well and was less likely to actively "bring her out" about herself and her own topics.[11] This suggests perpetuation of the traditional family roles in which males provide economic support in return for wifely attention and deference.

As in the family, men occupy the predominant attention-getting roles in the larger society. These include managerial roles such as politician and corporate executive, as well as the major professional roles such as doctor, lawyer, and university professor. All of these roles permit men to concentrate on themselves and to claim the focus of attention in their official interactions. They are roles in which the male typically has a coterie of attention-giving subordinates—characteristically female—who attend to his personal and job needs. Furthermore, they are roles whose symbolic value compel deference and respectful attention from clients and patients in work interaction.[12]

It must be noted that the roles of men in work and public life differ considerably depending on their social class. Men who are not in the dominant classes do not enter the privileged attention-getting roles and cannot typically expect attention or deference in work relations.[13] However, the roles of most male workers differ considerably from that of female workers because they require attention to machines or objects rather than people. The exceptions are such roles as staff aide or administrative assistant, which require an extreme personal attentiveness typically expected of females. Men in these positions must develop their capacities for giving attention more than other men and, like male secretaries or nurses, may experience contradictions between their work roles and their other male roles.

ATTENTION AND CHARACTER

Because women's roles are so different from men's, women are socialized to a particular psychology—one of attention-giving. In patriarchal cultures, females develop a social character of "other-orientation," which includes the attention-giving psychology, whereas males are socialized to the character type of "self orientation," which entails an attention-getting psychology.[14] While recent social changes encourage greater self-orientation among women, sexual socialization continues to emphasize an other-oriented model for the female personality and encourages an attention-giving psychology among women that "fits" their typical roles. An analysis of male and female character can illuminate further the special interactional responsibilities placed on women and the formal restrictions on their rights to seek attention for themselves.

Female Character: Other-Orientation and Attention-Giving
The idea that the socialized female character is "other-oriented" has been developed by many feminist writers, most notably Simone de Beauvoir. In *The Second Sex*, de Beauvoir distinguishes between the female mode of "being-for-the-other" and the male one of "being-for-the-self." An other-oriented person focuses on

the needs, concerns, and interests of others; the primary concern, face-to-face, is to accommodate and affirm them. In contrast, the self-oriented person concentrates primarily on himself and his own well-being; face-to-face, he seeks attention for himself.

The traditional "feminine" traits—sensitivity, warmth, sweetness, generosity, supportiveness, and responsiveness—are all expressions of other-orientation. Today, many men have these traits and many women do not. But women are still expected to acquire the basic elements of an attention-giving psychology. The "feminine" personality learns to share attention rather than seek it exclusively for herself.

This other-orientation is built on self-sacrifice and a requirement of underplaying her own needs in everyday interactions. Accordingly, women learn not only to give attention to others, but experience some degree of doubt, fear, or guilt when taking it or accepting it for themselves. Mary Rohman, in an unpublished study based on tape-recordings of women talking with each other about conversation, reported that many of the women interviewed admitted to seeking invisibility or a low profile in social interactions, particularly in conversations with men. Some feel they simply do not deserve attention, while others indicated that their socialization has led them to feel less feminine when they compete to bring attention to themselves.[15]

Rohman's findings suggest that the other-oriented woman is doubly disadvantaged psychologically. First, she must struggle with underlying doubts about her own rights to attention. Many females, from an early age, experience anxiety and guilt even in the simplest acts of asserting themselves for attention:

Even as a child I was afraid to compete for attention with my peers. As a child I was very invested in maintaining an image of gentle quietude, which I believe must have been forty percent fear. Learning to break through the quietude and passivity requires an act of faith and a certain amount of reassurance that it will be worth the discomfort. . . . [16]

Second, a woman's fears and doubts about taking attention are often linked to anxieties about femininity. A woman is in the unique position of having her sexual identity tied to the giving of attention. By giving it she validates her own femininity, not only in the eyes of males, who expect this behavior from her and reward her for it, but also frequently in her own eyes.

However, by seeking and taking attention, she can cast into doubt her feminine identity. If she competes aggressively with males, refusing to accept the expected attention-giving role, they may reject her sexually. Rohman quotes one woman as saying, "If I don't talk, it's because I know that a lot of the men will like me better for sexual kinds of reasons." Under these conditions, it may be easier for a woman to concede many of her own attention needs rather than place her sexual identity constantly in jeopardy.

Many women develop a specifically other-oriented way of seeking attention as a compromise between their needs for attention and their fear of demanding it directly. This is illustrated by one woman's description of how she learned to gain some attention in an encounter group:

I had spent most of the time observing and watching other people run the group. They seemed to have a definite ideal of what was happening and I certainly didn't, so I wasn't able to compete for attention in that area. I finally found my own attention device, although when I began to talk I felt extremely embarrassed and I could hear my voice shaking. I spoke about some changes in my own feelings about the group, but I spoke in terms of the entire group, rather than confining the observation to myself. It was a genuine observation—the first major one about the emotional state of the group itself—but it also served the purpose of drawing a distinct form of attention to myself. The group leader picked up on the generalization immediately and attempted to have me focus the observation back on myself. I felt that he had somehow seen through me and could tell that my good (encounter group) girl pose was no more than a ploy for attention.[17]

This nicely illustrates the other-oriented model of seeking attention. Attention is drawn indirectly to the self by speaking about others. The woman here gets visual attention by talking, while diverting topical attention to the group as a whole. Many women gain attention by talking about those with whom they are conversing (their children, husbands, etc.), thus winning attention while simultaneously focusing on others.

Male Character: Self-Orientation and Attention-Getting

Turning to male psychology, we find again a "fit" between social roles and character structure. The common male roles are attention-getting, encouraging the self-orientation central in American society. Two attributes of male psychology are (1) expecting in everyday interactions to be a focus of attention, and (2) being unable or unwilling to give more than civil attention.[18] These are ordinary, taken-for-granted attitudes reflecting subtle male privilege and power. Males are not openly taught that their sex entitles them to special claims to attention; in fact, they are more likely to be given instruction in the civilities of attending courteously and graciously to others, particularly to women. Yet this largely involves conformity to the ritual codes of civil attention and male chivalry and does not conflict with broader male self-orientation.

Just as women can validate their femininity by giving attention, men can affirm their feelings of masculinity by actively pursuing it. Males are generally socialized to a personality model that enables them to dominate attention; all the central masculine traits—aggressiveness, assertiveness, competitiveness, authoritativeness, self-assurance—are instrumental in gaining and maintaining attention. The following observation shows how "masculine" competitiveness and aggressiveness are advantageous in gaining attention in conversation:

> A man and a woman are sitting together at the bar intently absorbed in conversation. They both appear to be dynamic personalities, but he is more forceful and aggressive. He is doing most of the talking, most of it about himself; she does not appear resigned to the passive listening role and makes active efforts to enter the conversation. However, whenever they begin to talk at the same time, he persists aggressively, while she backs off. She makes no audible protest, but there is a flash of distress in her eyes each time this happens. On one occasion, she perseveres a little longer than usual, but he refuses to give way. He gives no sign he is aware she is trying to talk and simply raises his voice so it can be heard clearly over hers. Again, she sinks back silently in submission.

"Masculine" aggressiveness is here well adapted to the norms of individual initiative governing conversational attention.[19] Males are less bound than females by constraints on egoistic, self-assertive, or competitive behavior and so are free to take the kind of forceful initiative that can silence others, especially women. Their aggressiveness is often linked to self-assurance and authoritativeness, equally important in winning attention:

> A mixed group of six people are sitting and talking at a table in a restaurant. The person at the "top" of the attention-hierarchy is a man who is outgoing and sure of himself. He maintains eye contact with everyone talking to him, initiates conversations in which he knows a lot about the subject, and appears to know more about any subject brought up than anyone else in the group. He sustains his dominance by using words like "definitely," "I'm sure of

it," and "It's got to be that way because . . ." in a strong, sure tone of voice.[20]

Observers reported that males more frequently expressed themselves in this authoritative and assured manner, while females, often speaking in a hesitant or questioning tone of voice, were more likely to lose attention by showing uncertainty and lack of confidence.[21] This contrast reflects the underlying differences in socialized male and female character. Authoritativeness and self-assurances are central to the idealized masculine personality and are developed in boys through identification with cultural models of masculinity (such figures as John Wayne and Humphrey Bogart) and through traditional patterns of male socialization.[22]

Many males who are passive, quiet, or shy, while superficially less demanding of attention in ordinary interactions and less adequately equipped psychologically to claim it, have, nonetheless, been socialized to expect focal attention from women. Lacking the personal power to enforce their demands, they must rely more heavily on their public status or occupational position to secure attention. These men often impose an extra burden on women, as they expect no less attention than other males but demand that women play a more active role in assuring that they get it.[23]

INFORMAL INTERACTIONS: CONVERSATION BETWEEN THE SEXES

One can ask at this point whether the male attention-getting orientation and the female attention-giving orientation are expressed not only in formal interactions defined by their institutional roles but also in informal conversation in personal life. In Part I, we treated informal social life as a sphere in which social identities, inequalities, and roles are suspended and a pretense of equality among the participants is maintained. Were this strictly true, it would mean that men and women in many ordinary conversations are released from normal attention-getting and attention-giving expectations.

The restrictions on females taking attention and the assurances of males getting it are indeed far weaker in informal conversation than in formal interactions. Many women, by virtue of talkativeness, expressiveness, or emotional charisma, receive much attention in informal conversation and, unless they are extraordinarily domineering and competitive, do not face the same penalties they would elsewhere. Many women routinely compete over topics and display "conversational narcissism." Since this is the dominant American norm for informal behavior, women who constantly redirect the talk and attention to themselves do not necessarily experience the guilt, anxiety, or sense of threat to their femininity that constrains them in their formal interactions.

However, studies of everyday conversation suggest that the typical sex-role expectations are not completely suspended in informal social life. While status inequalities are less emphasized, people do not talk as socially neutral participants but as male and female conversationalists with different psychologies and different external constraints.[24] While women are permitted in informal conversations to be far more self-oriented than in their institutional roles, attention-giving is still defined mainly as a female responsibility and men are favored when competing for attention.

Support for this thesis comes from studies of the relative talking time in mixed groups, the topics most commonly discussed, patterns of interruption and deference, and the relative responsiveness of each sex to the other's ideas, feelings, and assertions. Studies of talking time do not sustain stereotypes of the "talkative female" and the "silent male." They indicate that men tend to speak more often and for longer periods of time, while women more frequently take the listening role.[25] (This has led feminists to suggest that the "talkative woman" is simply one who talks as much as a man.) Mary Rohman, in the study mentioned earlier, reports that many women say they are intimidated in male-female conversation and feel powerless to control the flow of conversation in groups of friends. Jessie Bernard, in reviewing anecdotal and available research evidence, concludes that it is somewhat unusual in a group for males to sit quietly and listen to females talking, while the reverse is much more common.[26]

Men are also more likely to control topics. Male-female conversation is more likely to focus on "male" topics, whether they be personal topics about the individual male speakers or more impersonal topics like sports, cars, or politics.[27] "Female" topics, including children, clothes, or emotions, are reserved for conversations among women.[28]

As suggested in the last chapter, most ordinary conversation is ego-centered, the topics having something to do with one or another of the conversationalists. While it is conventional wisdom, enshrined in etiquette books and popular advice columns, that it is the male prerogative to talk about himself and the responsibility of the woman to draw him out,[29] empirical studies suggest a more complex process takes place. In my study of dinner conversations I found that a substantial majority of the topics initiated by conversationalists were about themselves, with no significant differences in this regard between men and women.[30] However, other research suggests that females are more likely to be responsive to male initiatives, while males frequently respond in ways that undermine women's efforts to talk about themselves.[31] Men are particularly inclined to react with what I have called "minimal response" (see Chapter 1), a response that is not blatantly rude, but so small (such as "hmmm") as to induce doubt in the other about one's attention. Speaking up and pursuing their own topic is thus a greater risk for women, who often face the unpleasant choice of either remaining quiet or talking and feeling foolish or anxious about whether anyone is really listening.[32]

There is preliminary evidence that support-responses, responses that encourage the topics of others and do not cause a shift in attention back to the self, are sex-linked. In studies of dinner conversations I found that women are more likely to ask supportive questions. Drawing others out is a special skill associated with nurturance and mothering. It is also part of a feminine style which holds and attracts men. Most conversational studies suggest that listening is an essentially female skill. While listening is socially necessary, it is not generally rewarded in an individualistic, self-oriented culture. Women are expected to listen because of their subordinate status.[33] Given the prevailing culture, it is scarcely surprising that even many women violate these expectations; yet many others do learn to listen and these are held up as models for feminine behavior.

Nonetheless, women are free in many conversations to assume the talking role as well. Since male needs for attention are better met in their work and family roles, they are willing to cede women a certain measure of attention in sociability, where it costs them little and allows females to feel they are not being totally neglected. Women, on the other hand, cannot approach conversation so casually. The common opinion that women have a greater need to socialize and to talk reflects their greater attention deprivation in their institutional roles; women depend heavily on conversation as a compensatory arena. Extremely verbose women, who alienate others by talking constantly, have turned to the "proper" domain for attention but are unable to contain themselves within the prescribed latitudes.

As indicated earlier, even when women talk, it is often in ways that steer attention to others rather than themselves. As part of their other-orientation many women learn to feel a responsibility for the feelings of others in conversation and so act in ways that promote others' sense of well-being and security. Women talk to smooth over awkward silences, to ease latent conflicts, to make others feel at home, and to include people who are not being noticed. Moreover, a woman will often speak only when she senses a man does not wish to talk himself and wants her to take up the slack. She may quickly retreat when she receives a signal that he is ready to begin speaking.

Even when women seek attention for themselves by talking, talkativeness itself does not guarantee success. Patterns of ritualistic listening described in the last chapter, associated with nods of the head or minimal acknowledgments while thoughts are far from the conversation, is a common means by which males succeed in denying attention to talkative women. In families, talkative mothers are often "tuned out" by other family members.

The family is at dinner and the mother is talking all the time. She is talking mostly about her organizational work— what her current projects are and how they are coming along. She then begins talking about what she and her girlfriend from out of town did during the day. Everybody continued to eat and seemed, at best, to be listening halfheartedly. Occasionally, one of the others at the table would pop up with a question, almost as though it was required to show some sign of interest. While the mother talked, all the others looked down and were giving most of their attention to what was on their plates.

One of the most common complaints of wives is the reluctance of their husbands—lost behind their breakfast newspapers or their own internal preoccupations—to listen. Female talkativeness is often a response to male withdrawal and uncommunicativeness, creating a deteriorating cycle in which her increased talk leads only to being more ignored.

Under certain circumstances, normally involving either flirtation and sexuality or female helplessness and dependency, men do listen and accord women the attention-getting position. Girls learn early that males will give them attention on the basis of sexual interest and so learn to connect attention and sexuality far more closely than boys. Many come to believe that their sexuality is their most legitimate claim on attention and learn to view attention as a reward for pleasing men physically. This is reinforced by male attention-giving in conversation, which can vary erratically depending on sexual interest. Men who typically refuse the listening role often become highly attentive and conversationally responsive to women who are attractive to them. At the same time, they are likely to withdraw their attention and again focus on themselves when their sexual interests change or decline. This leaves women at the mercy of sexual dynamics which are often subterranean but create bizarre and disturbing shifts in the attention they receive. When a man gives a woman attention—even by listening attentively—she must, in many situations, immediately wonder whether he has sexual expectations; if he obviously does, she can feel comfortable taking more attention only if she expects to be sexually responsive. Women must constantly reassess the situation and consider whether by accepting attention from men they are consenting—or appearing to consent—to a hidden agenda that is not their own.

Being attentive and responsive to women who attract them sexually is one of the few forms of attention-giving in which men do not compromise their masculinity. While they are temporarily relinquishing their attention-getting prerogatives, they remain self-oriented and expect sexual rewards in return. Moreover, when a man affirms a woman in her sexuality, he is implicitly affirming his own sexuality, one of the few occasions in which the self-oriented male behaves with the recognition that affirmation of the other can be a way of affirming the self.

When sexuality is not a factor, men are most likely to accept a listening role if a woman presents herself as weak or helpless. The therapeutic model, in which a strong male gives attention to a weak female, extends beyond therapy to ordinary conversation. Men assume uncharacteristic listening postures toward women who send clear signals of vulnerability and distress. This kind of male attention stems from the chivalrous and patriarchal code that dictates masculine protection for a feminity that acknowledges its own dependency.

In therapy, the person who receives attention is less "powerful." This unusual separation of power and attention generally characterizes the circumstances under which men give attention to women. Unlike women, men do not normally give attention from a position of weakness or social inferiority but only when their own strength and power is being reaffirmed. This suggests why crying and other expressions of emotional distress are especially effective female ways of getting attention. A woman's tears are not only an open acknowledgment of her vulnerability, but a seductive invitation for the male to assume the position of strength that validates his masculinity.

This points to one of the few competitive advantages that women exercise in attention-getting. Although attention is not allocated according to need,[34] openly expressing need can be a powerful means of claiming it. The rules of civility described in the last chapter require that attention be given to those obviously in distress—and most people do respond in such cases, either out of politeness or genuine compassion. The greater freedom of women to cry, show vulnerability, or acknowledge helplessness is, other than sexuality, their strongest claim on attention.

The expectation that men do not cry or show their feelings is one of the most significant impediments to males getting attention. This is particularly the case for men socialized to a strict model of masculinity in which any expression of feeling is regarded as self-indulgent and any betrayal of need or insufficiency as effeminate. Such men are committed to an image of strength and self-control that can be easily interpreted as a disavowal of any need for attention and can discourage others from giving any they might otherwise be inclined to offer.

For some men, the requirements of masculinity lead not only to inhibition of weeping, but also inability to open up about personal difficulties, or even to talk about themselves at all. Such males frequently assume the role of therapist in their personal conversations, becoming uncommonly good listeners with women, but at the same time maintaining their sense of masculinity by identifying with the power of the therapist's role. However, the pretense that they have no needs and are fully in control of themselves can lead to a subtle form of attention-deprivation. Such men may share the subtle sense of oppression experienced by many women that they are constantly listening to the other sex without any real reciprocation.

Many men envy the female freedom to be openly emotional and vulnerable and covet the kind of attention it brings. Feminine emotionality, however, gives women only a limited advantage in claiming attention. As in the case of children, it is easily disparaged as "infantile" and used as a pretext for denying women attention. Except in special settings, women must generally limit their emotionality in social interactions in order to be taken seriously. Moreover, men, while handicapped by their lack of emotional expressiveness, can rely on the socialized skill of women to intuit and be responsive to their unacknowledged feelings and needs.

4 Attention for Sale: The Hidden Privileges of Class

[This chapter was co-authored with Dr. Yale Magrass.]

Suddenly, a sharp, dry cough was heard, and they all looked around. It came from a tall supercilious-looking Rocket, who was tied to the end of a long stick. He always coughed before he made any observation, so as to attract attention.

"Ahem, Ahem," he said, and everybody listened. . . . As soon as there was perfect silence, the Rocket coughed a third time and began. He spoke with a very slow distinct voice, as if he was dictating his memoirs, and always looked over the shoulder of the person to whom he was talking. In fact, he had a most distinguished manner. "I am a very remarkable Rocket, and come of remarkable parents. My mother was the most celebrated Catherine Wheel of her day, and was renowned for her graceful dancing. When she made her public appearance she spun around nineteen times before she went out and each time that she did so she threw into the air seven pink starts. My father was a Rocket like myself and of French extraction. He flew so high people were afraid that he would never come down. He did though, for he was of a kindly disposition, and he made a most brilliant descent in a shower of golden rain. . . ."

"I am made for public life," said the Rocket, "and so are all my relations. . . . Whenever we appear we excite great attention. . . ."

OSCAR WILDE, from "The Remarkable Rocket"

The proliferation of imitation status goods is powerful testimony to our on-going concern with making an impression. Counterfeiting has quadrupled over the last decade and is now estimated as a $200 million business. In the mid-1980s, it was estimated that the share of fakes on the U.S. market was 25 percent for designer sunglasses, more than 25 percent for watches, and 10 percent for jeans.

JULIET SCHOR, *The Overspent American*

What is at issue here, however, is the question: how far is commodity exchange together with its structural consequences able to influence the total outer and inner life of society?

GEORGE LUKACS, from *History and Class-Consciousness*

We have seen in the last chapter a close relation between attention and power. In America, wealth, occupation, and education all significantly affect who gets attention in everyday interactions, with members of privileged groups receiving the most and those in subordinate groups experiencing a certain daily invisibility. Inequalities of attention grow out of the most fundamental forms of social inequality and must be understood partly as a feature of a society divided into classes.

Socially dominant classes have the power to define themselves as having greater personal and social worth than those in inferior positions and thus more deserving of attention. They are best able to exhibit the prevailing societal symbols of worth, symbols described by Richard Sennett as "badges of ability" that all members of society accept as tangible measures of merit. By displaying these symbols, people affirm themselves in the eyes of others as individuals of special distinction, whose abilities and achievements give them unqualified claim to attention.[1] In stratified societies, dominant classes largely define these symbols and assign them to achievements and possessions reflecting their own class advantages.

In America, the dominant classes are those which come to

control economic, political, and cultural life. They include the monied class that owns economic resources and the emerging class of managers and professionals that exercises economic and cultural authority over the rest of the population. The subordinate classes include a marginal underclass comprising the poor, unemployed, and peripherally employed, and the working class whose members are employed but do not own capital or exercise authority.[2] Members of dominant classes have advantages in gaining attention in what we have called "formal" interactions principally because of their power and official status.[3] They monopolize the commanding attention-getting roles in cultural and political life and in workplaces. In addition, they are advantaged in informal interactions because wealth, occupation, and education create added claims to attention in ordinary conversations. We shall begin by considering the relation of attention to wealth—first in formal, then in informal interactions—and then consider how occupational roles and educational standing affect the attention any individual receives.

ATTENTION AS A COMMODITY: WEALTH AND THE PURCHASE OF ATTENTION

In modern industrial societies, a growing percentage of the individual's social life occurs in "secondary" relationships mediated by money and commercial interests. People must seek to satisfy their basic needs—including attention—in interactions governed directly or indirectly by the market. Attention has become increasingly available as a commodity to be purchased from people who give attention in the course of their work and expect to be paid for their services. Members of the dominant classes are best able to afford attention of this kind and consume the greatest amount.

Consider, for example, the purchase of attention in psychotherapy. Therapy is a market-based formal interaction explicitly structured to assure the client-purchaser most of the attention. In exchange for a fee, the client is assured that the only legitimate focus or "subject" of the interaction is herself. (The therapist who repeatedly seeks to introduce himself as the focus of attention violates the most fundamental norm of therapy.) The therapist is the quintessential professional attention-giver, for the focus of his training is the development of attention-giving skills and it is these skills for which he is paid.

In the therapeutic setting, unlike many other market settings, there is no subtlety cloaking the exchange of attention for money, as the therapist publicly offers his attention and the client openly purchases it. In the therapeutic process itself, however, the therapist must convince his client that he is giving his attention out of genuine concern and sympathy rather than for purely pecuniary ends or the therapeutic endeavor is likely to fail. This reflects the fact that people are most gratified by attention they believe others spontaneously choose to give. Thus, even people purchasing attention want to believe that the other is giving his attention freely rather than because his purchase requires it.

Psychoanalysis and psychotherapy continue to be a luxury enjoyed by business and professional classes. Members of subordinate classes can rarely afford to enter psychotherapy and so must seek other, and less expensive, forms of attention. The options are limited, however, as access to most of the attention-getting roles (and formal interactions) in the marketplace requires considerable money, and those roles which they may be able to afford offer less attention than those available to the privileged.

The purchase of attention in restaurants, a very different kind of market setting, illustrates this point well. Getting attention is part of the pleasure of "eating out," even in a modest restaurant where the amount of attention the customer can normally expect is limited to the simple serving of a meal.[4]

But the attention purchased in the expensive restaurant is distinct. The reputation of an exclusive restaurant rests not only in the quality of its food, but its capacity to deliver in delicately-structured interactions the extra attention for which its affluent clientele is presumably deserving and able to pay. Consider the following observation:

> We were greeted by the owner himself, who was dressed in extremely formal attire, but welcomed us informally, as if he were personally pleased to see us. All through the meal, one waiter hovered over our table watching to see if we needed anything. He moved quickly to fill our glasses and to make sure that we had the right sauces and condiments. The head waiter had a distinguished manner, with the expected French accent, and was extremely deferential. In taking our orders, he spoke softly and unobtrusively, yielding the floor immediately whenever one of us began to speak. He was responsive to our inquiries, showing considerable knowledge of gastronomy, but careful not to draw too much attention to himself. He listened solicitously to each person's order, nodding supportively or appreciatively at the selections and never allowing his gaze to wander. All staff members were, in fact, extremely attentive. The wine stewards, busboys, and waiters also approached us respectfully and served the food with a sense of exquisitely concentrated care and concern.[5]

Here, the role of customer is a source of exceptional attention. The patron purchases the services of a variety of attention-givers, as well as the rights to a carefully cultivated face-to-face deference. He can immediately engage those serving him[6] and, in face-to-face interaction, can expect unhurried and uninterrupted attention. These waiters[7] are trained to give undivided visual attention, to listen solicitously, and to refrain from making themselves the focus of the interaction. This can involve considerable finesse, as in the case of the headwaiter, who is expected to speak with a certain elegance befitting an attendant of a distinguished patron but not in a style that calls undue notice to himself.

The waiter-patron interchange in the expensive restaurant reflects the way attention is typically allocated in formal interactions, with people in the dominant classes gaining the attention and members of the subordinate classes giving it. Since attention-giving is related to offering deference and respect, the transaction not only reflects the economic power of those in the giving and getting roles, but symbolically affirms their relative social worth.[8]

The privileged classes purchase attention not only in restaurants, shops, and other public settings, but also in formal interactions in private life, by employing attention-givers in the home. As depicted in chronicles of upper-class life, such as the popular television series "Upstairs, Downstairs," members of the dominant classes have historically surrounded themselves with servants recruited from the subordinate classes who must routinely give attention to whomever pays for their services. Even in the contemporary affluent household, cooks, cleaning ladies, governesses, and other domestic help are employed in attention-giving roles and are judged partly by the quality of the attention they give.[9] In many upper-class homes, liveried servants continue to serve dinner, while valets and chauffeurs attend to the adults. The privileged classes are also able to purchase "overseers" (nannies, governesses, etc.) for their children, thus relieving parents of many attention-giving responsibilities.

WEALTH AND INFORMAL INTERACTIONS: ATTENTION AND CONSUMPTION DISPLAYS

Attention is "purchased" in a different way in the informal interactions of everyday life. By displaying symbols of material success, an individual can increase his sense of his own worth and his rights to attention, while at the same time predisposing others to give the attention expected. Ostentatious or subtle exhibits of property can be used both to attract attention in public places and to help a person maintain the focus of attention in everyday conversations.[10]

Displays of clothing are the most important evidences of property in ordinary interaction. Dressing fashionably is an extremely common means by which people seek to gain attention. Here, members of the dominant classes are especially advantaged, as they define style and can best afford to dress glamorously. For example:

> Two women were sitting over lunch in the restaurant associated with the museum. A third woman, elegantly coiffured and stylishly dressed, sat down to join them. In greeting her, her friends immediately focused their attention on her, looking intently at her outfit and commenting on how lovely she looked. Both commented specifically about her dress and she began to talk at some length about the dress itself and her experiences in shopping for it. The other women, after a few minutes, began to try to broaden the conversation and bring in some of their own shopping experience. By returning to one or another feature of the very striking dress she was wearing, the woman who had been dominating the conversation continued to redirect the conversation to her own clothes and experiences in shopping. The others subsided into a permanent listening role, only letting their attention wander occasionally when they scrutinized the outfits of other elegantly dressed women who were walking by.

Here, a stylish woman focuses the conversation on herself by referring constantly to her clothes. Clothing has special importance for women, who are taught to seek attention through glamor and sexuality. Moreover, women in the dominant classes can use their economic resources to gain added advantages not available to less affluent women in daily interactions. While the latter also learn to rely heavily on clothing to gain attention, they cannot normally afford the expensive jewelry, elegant wardrobes, and other glamorous or very stylish items that win privileged women extra attention.[11]

The automobile is another possession that symbolizes social worth and is "displayed" to bring attention to the self. By driving such luxury cars as Cadillacs, Continentals, Mercedes, and Rolls Royces, wealthy individuals attract attention in the streets and in public places.[12] One millionaire's "outsize white Cadillac with a gold plated dashboard" has been described by C. Wright Mills as a lavish example from an earlier era. Nowadays, the acquisition of expensive but less blatantly garish vehicles, including sports cars, antique automobiles, and chauffeured limousines, remains a means by which dominant groups indirectly "purchase" attention.[13]

There are many other areas in which dominant groups set standards of taste and draw attention by displays of consumer sophistication. Tasteful displays of furniture, art work, glassware, china and cutlery, stereophonic equipment, and other household items are used by members of affluent groups as subtle ways of establishing their worth and rights to special attention in everyday interactions.

In consumer economies, through advertising, members of subordinate classes also learn to depend on clothes, cars, and other consumer goods as attention-getting commodities. Advertising successfully persuades consumers that without certain products they will appear either ugly, uncultivated, or offensive, leading others to withdraw attention. Listerine ads warn people of the consequences of bad breath, cosmetic ads condemn unsightly, pimpled, or wrinkled skin. Buying commodities thus helps reduce personal anxieties about getting attention; if most members of the society cannot afford to buy the clothes and other expensive goods to make them fashionable or "glamorous" like the upper classes, at least they can avoid the "blemishes" that might mar their appearance by making relatively inexpensive consumer purchases.[14]

Subordinate groups also buy goods to attract desirable attention. A given toothpaste will buy a winning smile with sparkling white teeth; a given perfume will attract and hold the attention of that glamorous man in the office. People in the subordinate classes, without access to institutional attention-getting roles, may come to depend especially on the acquisition of goods to compensate. The worker in the factory and the clerk in the office who get little or no attention in their work roles may be able to afford the flashy car, clothes, and other goods that bring some attention in personal interaction. While for many consumption is one of the few avenues for gaining attention, it is part of a system that best serves the privileged classes, as they can purchase the commodities which most symbolize worth.

We have examined some of the ways in which monied groups purchase attention in formal interactions and in everyday social life. One further point about the relation between money and attention, particularly in regard to the poor,[15] deserves discussion. We suggested earlier that the attention-getting role is normally the powerful one,[16] but there are exceptions affecting mainly the poor. A number of institutions, including welfare agencies, social work offices, and employment services, offer poor people roles in which they receive face-to-face attention. However, power in these interactions rests in the hands of those giving attention. Welfare client, as an example, is a role of weakness and helplessness, bringing attention at the cost of respect and requiring that the individual acknowledge personal incapacity, failure, or dependency.

Under these conditions, the attention-getting role is one the individual would ordinarily avoid. Those receiving such attention are less likely to feel supported or nurtured as intruded upon, violated, or humiliated. They have little control over the nature of the interaction and the attention given, or over how the parts of their personalities and life histories are examined and revealed.

While attention is always potentially controlling or victimizing, this is especially true when the attention-giver represents social control agencies. Giving attention becomes part of the exercise of power and the attention itself a threat or weapon.[17]

ATTENTION AND WORK

In addition to being a commodity that can be purchased, attention is a reward of authority and prestige in work. People in the dominant occupations[18] gain special attention in the formal interactions in their work life and also in their informal interactions in personal life. This is related both to the structure of work roles and to the growing importance of work as the governing symbol of social worth.

The claim to expertise is a primary source of power for those in dominant occupations and a formidable way of gaining attention. People approach most professionals for what they believe is valuable information and not only pay generously for it, but give in return an uncommonly close form of attention.[19] The worried patient will hang on every word of his doctor, the legal client will listen keenly to the advice of his lawyer, the avid student will give undivided attention to the professor who knows what the student wants to know. Professionals frequently use "displays" of knowledge to capture attention:

This professor had an air of expertise that was extremely effective in capturing and holding the attention of his students. During the lecture, he referred constantly to the books he had written, as well as the one he was currently writing. These references seemed to have an effect, as students whose attention had been wandering refocused their gaze on him at these points.

More subtle displays are also common:

The teacher is unpretentious and one of those rare instructors who makes it clear that he is not an absolute expert in the field. He confesses this fact frequently during the class. Laughing it off, he gains power and attention by giving the tacit implication that he knows more than he would admit to. Students keep their eyes riveted on him and do not stare out the window, whisper to each other or show other signs of diverted attention.

A professional is normally granted attention automatically on the basis of assumed expertise and knowledge. A resort to conscious "displays," even of the subtle kind illustrated here, is thus likely to happen only under those circumstances—which occur frequently in the classroom—where the professional is uncertain that those required by their role to listen to him are actually doing so.[20]

The control of rewards and punishments also assures professionals and managers attention in formal interactions. In a courtroom, all parties extend respectful attention to the judge, not only because of the ritual formalities but because of the inordinate power he or she wields over the fate of the petitioners.[21] Similarly, at the workplace, because the employer hires and fires and controls conditions of work, employees focus on her. In face-to-face interactions with his boss, a subordinate must give respectful attention even if he feels resentment or bitterness. This is a part of deference in formal interactions: the role of the subordinate is not only to listen and respond to instructions or commands, but also to show respect by being especially attentive and taking care not to draw undue attention to himself.[22]

Professional services have traditionally required attention-giving to clients in face-to-face interactions.[23] More recently, however, changes in professional work roles have shifted attention-giving responsibility from professionals to less skilled subordinates; the professional spends less of his time in interactions with clients and, during the time he does so, often gains attention as the "expert" rather than giving it as a helper. These changes are well illustrated in the following observation in a private hospital room:

The patient is resting in a single room two days after abdominal surgery. She is seen primarily by nurses and aides who enter the room every couple of hours to check vital signs and the I.V. The major attending nurse is solicitous and personally attentive. In the early afternoon she enters and asks how the patient is feeling. The patient smiles and indicates she is feeling stronger. She then says she is feeling more pain around the incision. She describes the pain and the nurse listens attentively. The nurse sits on the bed and feels carefully around the abdominal area. She touches her gently and with some nurturance. She tells the patient there is no indication of infection or other problems, but she should let her know about any acute pain that develops. She is reassuring and supportive. She also indicates that the doctor, whom the patient has seen only once since the operation, will be coming to see her in the afternoon.

The doctor arrives an hour later. He is friendly, but formal and personally remote. He asks how the patient is doing; as she answers, he does not look at her but at a chart he is holding. He asks her a few questions in quick succession, now looking at the patient, but indicating by his manner that he does not have much time. She then asks quickly about her abdominal condition. She is interested in the exact prognosis of the disorder. He then begins a rather lengthy, authoritative description of the disease. He seems to enjoy talking about it and expounds on it for about five minutes. The attention in the interaction remains clearly focused on him for the rest of the time, and he leaves right after his exposition.

The difference in the two interactions is striking. With the nurse, the focus of attention remains on the patient and the nurse exhibits a "bedside manner" traditionally associated with family doctors. The doctor, on the other hand, interacts with the patient less as a caretaker than as expert consultant. In the "expert" role he becomes the focus of attention himself and offers relatively little attention to the patient.

The same dynamics are evident in higher education. Professors are "experts" who meet with students in large classes to impart knowledge. To the extent that students receive any attention, they are less likely to receive it from their professors in the classroom than from teaching assistants or graduate students who lead discussion groups, read papers, and meet with students in individual consultations. Like nurses and medical paraprofessionals, teaching assistants are part of an emerging stratum of subordinates who buffer professionals from demands of clients and take over the routine burden of attention-giving.

In the business world executives and bosses also delegate much of the responsibility of attention-giving to subordinates. The secretary-receptionist, for example, not only gives attention to clients, but must do so in a way conducive to her boss's interests. Secretaries give attention to their bosses as well as to clients, nurses to doctors as well as patients, and teaching assistants to professors as well as to students. These attention-givers thus benefit those in dominant occupations doubly, not only by lightening their attention-giving responsibilities but reinforcing their attention-getting status.[24]

INVISIBILITY AT WORK: SUBORDINATE OCCUPATIONS

The work roles of those not in dominant occupations are rarely attention-getting ones. Most sales and service workers, clerical workers, and industrial workers do not have subordinates expected to give them attention. The only attention that these workers can typically expect in their formal interactions is from supervisors who regulate their behavior.[25]

It is useful to distinguish subordinate workers who remain visible and others who become invisible. Invisibility, as R. D. Laing has pointed out, is the most drastic form of attention-deprivation, ultimately more painful and dehumanizing than hostile or other "negative" attention. Anyone can become temporarily invisible in meetings, groups, and other kinds of everyday situations. But for those whose job is regarded as dirty, unpleasant, or unsightly, and are therefore required to work in hidden places such as kitchens or basements, it is routine to their daily experience. Other workers of very low status, such as the cleaning lady or the busboy, while they may work in the purview of other people, remain invisible because others feel no need to acknowledge their presence.[26]

Erving Goffman's distinction between "front" and "back" regions of the workplace provides a basis for looking more closely at the difference between visible and invisible work roles. Goffman points out that work space can be divided into that accessible to the public or other outsiders (the "front" space) and those accessible only to the employees themselves (the "back" region). In a restaurant, the kitchen and stockroom are the back regions, while the dining room is the front region. There are normally physical barriers between front and back regions, designed to prevent those in the front regions from seeing what takes place in the back regions. Certain workers, such as waitresses, have access to both regions while others, such as dishwashers, are confined to the back region.

Goffman was primarily concerned with understanding work as a kind of performance and considered the back region as a backstage where the actors prepare the props and mobilize themselves for the drama in the front region. For our purposes, the distinction between front and back regions is useful in understanding who gives and gets attention. Those restricted to the front region can never give or get attention from those restricted to the back region and vice-versa.

Workers restricted to the back regions become invisible to the public. The kitchen help, for example, remains completely unseen by the clientele of the restaurant. Similarly, stockboys, packers, inventory clerks, and many clerical workers, who are normally restricted to back regions of department stores, grocery stores, and other service or retail establishments, also work unnoticed.

Being in an invisible work role does not imply that the worker gets no attention at all in his job. The dishwasher may seek and get attention in informal interactions with fellow workers in his back region. Moreover, he is freed from having to give attention to the clientele. Nonetheless, his invisibility to the public is symbolic of his low worth and disadvantages him in gaining attention.[27] Symbolically, it suggests that he is not entitled to acknowledgment or recognition from the clientele.

Workers confined to the back regions are not the only ones in invisible work roles. A more extreme form of dehumanization is experienced by those who work in front regions but whose presence commands no attention whatsoever. The sweeper in the restaurant, for example, carries out his work in full view without anyone else noticing him and remains unseen unless he commits an offense which violates his role. In the movie *Charlie*, for example, the hero, a busboy, is portrayed in his invisible role until he drops and breaks a stack of dishes, thus exploding out of his invisible position. Similarly, transportation workers and the janitors and groundskeepers in many establishments carry out their work in view of others and yet receive minimal recognition. A cleaning lady, or other domestic servants, may glide through the house performing her duties almost as a ghost, without family members taking any note of her presence.[28]

On the other hand, there are many work settings where the lower-status employees occupy the front regions while those with the greatest power are sheltered in exclusive back regions. In a bank, for example, the tellers are visible, while the executives are hidden within imposing offices. Similarly, in many bureaucracies, clerks and other low-status office workers can normally be seen within a large office space while the more powerful employees gradually disappear into asylums as they move up the ranks. In these circumstances, "invisibility" is actually a symbol of status. The executive suite is, however, a very different kind of back region from, say, the restaurant kitchen, and the "invisibility" of the high official is radically distinct from that of the dishwasher. The executive office is designed to serve the interest of the one who occupies it, functioning in many ways as a sanctuary from the demands of others. Moreover, the executive is invisible only when he chooses, as he has a staff of subordinate attention-givers (secretaries, personal aides, etc.) on whom he can call at any time. He also has access to the front region and can demand, if he desires, a great deal of attention from subordinates when he enters there.

Workers available to the public, moreover, such as bank tellers and receptionists, are normally in attention-giving roles. They typically receive from the public only the minimal acknowledgment of their presence that is required to conduct business. Their visibility merely reflects the obligation of giving attention to customers—a duty delegated to those in the front region—and not the privilege of receiving it, which is reserved for those in the back region.

As indicated earlier, all lower-status workers are assured, however, of getting the one kind of attention that all work establishments direct toward their employees, even the least favored in formal interactions: supervisory attention.[29] Employers extend the attention required to ensure that they are doing their job, maintaining discipline, and working at the rhythm and efficiency expected of them. On the assembly line, the foreman focuses his attention on the workers to regulate their behavior and prevent interruptions of the production process. The gaze of the foreman is the immediate expression, face-to-face, of a larger system of social control that institutionalizes the power of the employer over the worker; it is the most important and least desired of the forms of attention that workers receive.

WORK IDENTITY AND INFORMAL INTERACTION

We have seen that the competition for attention in ordinary informal interaction involves a struggle by each individual to establish his or her relative worth. High occupational status has become one of the most important symbols defining personal worth in ordinary social relations. As a result, professionals, executives, and others in dominant occupations enjoy a significant advantage in seeking and winning attention in ordinary conversation.

The importance of occupational status derives from the primacy of "ability" as a contemporary measure of worth. Richard Sennett has shown that ability (and accomplishment) has become a universal value that significantly affects the appraisal of members of all classes of their own worth and that of others. Occupational status is considered in modern culture the most tangible and compelling measure of ability and now carries the symbolic significance that wealth had in an earlier period.[30]

To exploit occupational status as a means of getting attention, the individual must successfully display or communicate it to others. Obviously, a doctor cannot expect special attention in conversation unless he has made his professional identity known. Unlike a property display, disclosures of occupational identity are not usually communicated visually (although a doctor, for example, can give visual cues by wearing a "beeper" or his white coat when off the job). Such information normally surfaces in conversation either by being openly discussed or by being subtly communicated through use of technical language or knowledge. A doctor's professional identity will normally become apparent to strangers or acquaintances when he talks directly about his work, uses some kind of medical vocabulary, or steers the discussion to health-related topics in which he has expertise. At the beginning of conversations between strangers or new acquaintances, people normally break the ice with the familiar question "What do you do?" Occupation is thus revealed at the outset and helps to establish the relative status of the parties talking and the allocation of attention.

In most social relations, those in dominant occupations need not disclose this information, as it is already known to family, friends, and others with whom they regularly interact. As such, their occupational status is a permanently recognized "badge of ability" that establishes their special worth in the eyes of others and, in most informal situations, enhances their perceived rights to attention. As indicated earlier, fathers in high status jobs often gain added attention in their families because of the prestige they carry from the outside world. Those who cannot exhibit the occupational "badge" or whose occupational status is clearly inferior, will find their worth constantly in question. In order to win attention, they must struggle to establish it in other ways. This is reflected in subtle dynamics in conversations among people of different occupational statuses. People of low status may feel the pressure to talk constantly simply to prevent others from withdrawing their attention altogether. This is reflected in the stereotypical "talkativeness" of housewives, who cannot draw on occupational status to secure attention in ordinary situations. An analysis of the talk of working-class housewives indicates that their lack of occupational status forces them to seek alternative strategies (obsessive talking is one possibility) to mitigate the fear that they might be completely disregarded.[31]

ATTENTION AND EDUCATION

An individual's education also has a major effect on the attention he receives in everyday interactions. Since access to higher education depends on one's class position[32] and is instrumental in one's gaining entry to dominant occupations, it becomes an indirect basis for access to the attention-getting roles already considered. In addition, independently of one's occupation and income, one's education can be a powerful claim on attention. In everyday conversation, people with college or advanced education have a number of advantages in gaining attention, stemming from the importance of schooling as a unique symbol of worth that entitles the individual to special forms of recognition.

This is partly due to the widespread tendency to equate schooling with intelligence. Intelligence is regarded as a fundamental kind of ability which commands enormous respect in contemporary culture, and its appearance or apparent absence has a major effect on the kinds of attention any individual receives. While there is no compelling evidence that those given special access to higher education are more intelligent than others, they are normally regarded as such, in part because education provides resources (mainly verbal skills and specialized information) for appearing so. Those without advanced education are widely considered deficient both in ability and intelligence, and thus lacking a claim to the interest and attention of others.

Education is also a badge or symbol of "self-development," another contemporary measure of worth, related to ability but more explicitly concerned with the extent to which talents, skills, and faculties have been cultivated and actualized (in a sense, the extent to which ability has been realized). The criterion of self-development means that those perceived as most "evolved" or "accomplished" are viewed as especially deserving of attention.[33]

Revelations about educational status are enormously important in shaping others' assessments of one's worth and regulating the flow of attention. People in dominant classes rely on their education as a major sign both of their "self-development" and their special rights to attention. Whenever the rights are in doubt, educated individuals will normally act to reaffirm their worth, often by displaying some expression of self development or schooling. This display can be compared to the property or consumer display described earlier, by which individuals exhibit evidence of wealth. One does not ordinarily make explicit reference to educational accomplishments, although an individual who offhandedly mentions his undergraduate experience at Princeton or the fact that he has a Ph.D. will enhance his status. Usually, the display is more subtle and indirect, involving either the use of sophisticated vocabulary and manner of speaking or the display of specialized knowledge.

Speech is enormously important as an education display and attention-getting cue. Sociolinguists have accumulated considerable evidence that people can be identified in terms of class, subculture, and education on the basis of how they talk.[34] Such matters as vocabulary, grammar, intonation, and diction significantly affect how people respond to one another. Members of dominant classes use an expanded vocabulary (including more technical, literary, or simply "big" words) as well as the "proper" or "standard" grammar and diction that others recognize as evidence of advanced schooling. Members of subordinate classes are likely to find themselves at a disadvantage when seeking attention in any face-to-face setting in which people of different classes are brought together. On the basis of speech patterns and other cues of educational background and class position, their ideas are less likely to be taken seriously, and others are less disposed to cede air time or listen attentively to them. Studies in such diverse contexts as jury rooms, parent-teacher meetings, and community gatherings indicate that those who talk the most frequently and whose ideas are given the greatest attention are invariably individuals with high educational status and class background, and that those less educated normally speak less often and receive less attention.[35]

Members of subordinate classes who do not exhibit the "standard" vocabulary, grammar, and diction are handicapped as soon as they begin to speak. These handicaps begin early in life, since the working- or lower-class child is less likely to get attention from teachers in school because of the way he talks.[36] This experience is reproduced in adult life in most organizations and institutions; bureaucrats, employers, and others in positions of authority, attuned to the class symbols of worth, are likely to direct attention preferentially on the basis of speech cues indicating education and class status. This is one of the most subtle forms of discrimination by class, reproduced in the everyday interactions within all our institutions.

5 On One's Own The Overburdened Self and the Need for Attention

We know well enough that the isolation of the individual—a narrow minded egotism—is everywhere the fundamental principle of modern society. . . . The disintegration of society into individuals each guided by his private principles and each pursuing his own aims, has been pushed to its furthest limits. . . .

FREDERICK ENGELS, from *The Condition of the Working-Class in England*

The compulsive preoccupation with being seen, or simply with being visible, suggests that we must be dealing with underlying fantasies of not being seen, of being invisible.

R. D. LAING, from *The Divided Self*

Paradise is gone for good; the individual stands alone and faces the world. . . .

ERICH FROMM, from *Escape From Freedom*

I have described dehumanizing patterns of interaction and attention-behavior. To consider how change in these patterns might occur, several essential questions must be asked. To what degree can the allocation of attention be cooperative and mutually supportive rather than competitive? To what extent can a psychology oriented toward giving attention be realized? Can inequalities in the distribution of attention be altered and definitions of social worth changed so that no group is regarded as unworthy of attention?

For such changes in everyday behavior to occur, the larger

society itself must be transformed. Attention-dynamics are shaped by cultural values, character structure, and the distribution of power. I have emphasized that the allocation of attention inevitably mirrors the basic structure of the society in which it evolves; it can thus assume a new form only if fundamental social change occurs.

The two central patterns in America—the competitive seeking of attention and the allocation of attention to socially dominant groups—subtly reflect the prevailing individualism and class structure. We have seen that competitiveness for attention mirrors broader forms of competition, just as inequalities of attention follow wider social inequalities. It is these roots in the larger society that need more explicit consideration.

I have discussed how attention-behavior in informal social life bears a strong resemblance to behavior in the marketplace: that is, each individual takes initiative on his own behalf with only minimum concern for the well-being of others. Such individualism is rooted in cultural norms extending far beyond attention-behavior. In the economic arena, individual initiative and responsibility for oneself are fundamental imperatives. Where norms of self-interest govern economic behavior, face-to-face social behavior is also invariably egoistic and competitive. While cultures are never totally integrated, a society cannot—without great tension—create demands of competitive behavior in the economic sphere and cooperative behavior in social life. The internalization of economic rules of self-interest breeds a psychological readiness to act egoistically even in the most intimate arenas of personal life. Such economic conditioning of psychological activity has been recognized by many theorists, most notably Erich Fromm, who has used such notions as the "marketing personality" to illustrate the influence of the capitalist system on psychology and personal relations.[1]

The self-orientation that pervades American social character is rooted in a "social" individualism that grows out of economic individualism: each person functions as an independent, isolated "self," whose survival and success depend on his own resources. With few exceptions, all people exist apart from any encompassing community upon which their fortunes depend. Since the individual is thrown onto his own resources, he must of necessity be primarily focused on himself and on satisfying his own needs.[2] Let us look more closely, then, at the ways in which such social atomization (or "disaffiliation") render the individual less willing and capable of giving attention and more needy and desirous of taking it.

SELF-ORIENTATION AND "SOCIAL" INDIVIDUALISM: THE INDIVIDUAL ON HER OWN

Insecurity underlies the attention-psychology of the self-oriented individual, an insecurity rooted in aloneness, the necessity of achieving self-sufficiency economically and socially, and the imperative of demonstrating uniqueness and special merit as an individual. As Fromm has suggested, people in an individualistic society experience feelings ranging from vague apprehension to acute panic about their economic and social isolation and their capacity to cope without community support. This insecurity intensifies preoccupation with oneself and has a major bearing on face-to-face behavior. It heightens one's own needs for attention and reduces the ability to give it, as one becomes riveted on one's own needs and fears.

Aloneness heightens the need for attention simply as a consequence of social deprivation. Notwithstanding the cultural ethos of "togetherness," individualistic society has increasingly transformed everyday life into isolated, privatized pursuits in which individuals learn to act and spend time alone. This is reflected in the increasing number of single people and in the new pervasiveness of privatized leisure pursuits, such as watching television, over such social activities as games or simple conversation. Because they are engaged in fewer activities with others, many people develop intensified needs for attention. An extreme example is the elderly, left alone for long periods. The self-oriented character, when entering the company of others, typically craves attention and redirects it to himself or herself.

Yet it is not simply lack of social contact but the burdens of coping on one's own that contribute most powerfully to insecurity and yearning for attention. Since the individual lacks enduring group or community support, she attempts to transform each individual encounter into a support vehicle that can compensate for her underlying vulnerability. She is impelled to seek attention to alleviate exacerbated daily stresses and difficulties—an approach that must fail not only because interactions with other disaffiliated persons can never provide the community support she seeks, but also because each self-oriented person seeks the attention the other requires.

Yet another factor is the precarious sense of worth experienced in individualistic societies. Each person's basic value is conditional upon his demonstrating his uniqueness and particular merit. The cultural pressures to prove one's distinctive individuality, and thus to claim one's moral rights as a full person, lead Americans to labor under the apprehension that they may not be regarded as worthy or acceptable by others, and induce a profound insecurity.[3] Under individualism, the person becomes self-oriented, then, because his value is so deeply in question. The culture perpetually redirects him to a focus on his own individuality, while simultaneously heightening his insecurity regarding his merit and worth as a developed being. The self inevitably becomes an object of concern and preoccupation, a form of "negative egoism" that typifies self-oriented characters in America.

This conditionality of worth places people in continuing doubt about their own rights to attention. This anxiety may include the fear that one is not sufficiently interesting to merit attention, a feeling that reflects the need to demonstrate excitement and uniqueness. While with women this uneasiness is displayed as apprehension about taking attention, it leads also to persistent efforts to gain recognition. The more one doubts one's worth or magnetism, the more important it becomes to claim attention and thereby set one's fears to rest. The self-oriented person thus persistently seeks attention, yet can never completely alleviate his doubts that he is entitled to it.

SELF-ORIENTATION AND
ECONOMIC INDIVIDUALISM

In America, economic forces and burdens lie at the heart of self-orientation. People are cut adrift from any community providing economic security. Thrown into a labor market that rewards individual performance while making employment precarious and highly competitive, each individual must become self-oriented simply to subsist and succeed.

Industrialization and capitalism imposed this economic individualism as earlier forms of community life were left shattered by the growth of the marketplace and private property and capital. Capitalism removed the control over economic life from the community, thus precipitating the decline of collectivity and the rise of the disaffiliated "self."[4] Simultaneously, it implanted within the individual both real and imagined individualistic notions that one's economic destiny was to be determined by one's own efforts.

Once communal beings were thus transformed into atomized agents on the labor market. As Fromm and others have stressed, tradition had previously bound the individual tightly to the community, closely regulating his economic behavior and responsibilities; while restricted in his freedom and mobility, each person had a security, assured by community support and cooperation. In the new capitalist labor market, the individual was on his own. His fate was determined by his own success in selling his skills or wares. Since his relations with others were now competitive rather than cooperative, he could no longer expect group support; the burdens of survival were now his alone.

Such economic individualism bred a new focus on self. Bearing sole responsibility for one's economic fate places a fundamental strain on psychic life, resulting in intensified concern with oneself and one's own fortunes. This is another form of "negative egoism," to be interpreted not as self-celebration but a response to acute insecurity. With his attention focused on economic preoccupations and anxieties, the individual has limited ability to give attention to others in everyday interactions; his resources overtaxed, he seeks attention without capacity for reciprocation.

The capitalist marketplace, while transforming survival from a collective to an individual preoccupation, simultaneously institutionalized mobility and the dream of self-aggrandizement. In economic life, mobility induces self-orientation, for it requires sustained attention to one's own advancement. The "mobile" self is the most disaffiliated, as mobility necessarily loosens the individual's ties to community. Dreams of advancement indeed presuppose a consciousness of a separate "selfhood" not highly developed in earlier eras. The mobility institutionalized by the marketplace slowly transforms the meaning of social identity itself from a secure and traditionally defined status in community to the personally defined and achieved "self."

Self-orientation becomes the consciousness of those most mobile and therefore least integrated in the community. Economically, it is expressed through such institutions as the "career," which are ways of organizing motivation and attention around the aims of the self. Particularly in the dominant classes, where prospects for mobility are strongest, careerism and visions of economic and social aggrandizement become the basis of an intensified self-absorption, while in subordinate classes, where vestiges of community (such as neighborhood and church) are stronger, self-orientation is less developed.

Within the dominant classes, economic self-orientation is

readily visible in the attention-dynamics of everyday interaction. Among the most career oriented, topics of conversation revert invariably to one's work, achievements, and difficulties. Conversational narcissism takes the form of establishing whose career circumstance is more deserving of attention. Underlying these dynamics is a profound need to gain attention and support for a "self" excessively vulnerable because of its dissaffiliation and lack of community support.

PROSPECTS FOR CHANGE: SOME SPECULATIONS ON THE FUTURE OF INDIVIDUALISM

The prospects for the erosion of self-orientation and egoistic attention-behavior are linked to reducing individualism. America is developing, however, not toward greater community or cooperation, but toward an intensification of the entrenched individualism. The continuing decline of the family, the neighborhood, and other "community" institutions along with the strengthening of capitalist values and institutions suggests the yet further ensnarement of the individual in the conditions originally creating his self-orientation: she is now no less responsible for her own economic fate but increasingly cut adrift from any permanent group that can support her socially. One would anticipate, then, a heightening of self-orientation and the even greater diffusion of the dehumanizing patterns of social interaction that we have described.

The deepening individualism and the potent self-orientation it evokes can be seen in contemporary cultural ideologies of "self-development" and "self-actualization." Under conditions of extreme individualism, the self becomes not simply a major but a primary focus of interest, and an ideology of self-cultivation takes root in large sectors of the population (normally the most individualized). This is associated, as Philip Reiff has brilliantly shown, both with the decline of any loyalty or attachment to community and the rise of a privatized "therapeutic" culture. Each individual is preoccupied with his own "personal growth" and increasingly incapable of transcending a highly complex but intensified egocentricity.[5]

While those within such a culture are oriented toward "personal relationships" requiring some giving of attention, the overriding commitment to oneself perpetuates the individualistic attention-dynamics. The therapeutic culture only exacerbates, in fact, the egoistic tendencies built into society, as it legitimates, on the basis of a sophisticated psychological ideology of self-actualization, the absorption of one's attention on oneself.

The growth of more humane face-to-face behavior is thus dependent on changes in society contrary to existing trends and improbable in the short run. Spiraling individualism and the intensification of self-orientation may continue, however, only until the effects of excessive individualization (and egoism) rebound so strongly against social community and the individual herself that counteracting tendencies emerge. As Philip Slater has suggested, changes in the key features of the culture, such as its individualism, cannot be simply legislated (despite the enormous importance of changes in the economic system that can facilitate it), but metamorphoses nonetheless can occur in response to crises generated in the society and culture. Crises in the economy, in the breakdown of social and community life, and in the mental health of individuals, all reflecting excessive individualism,[6] are likely to lead in the long run to a strengthening of latent economic, social, and psychological impulses toward collectivity and a diminishing of individualism.

The problem of how attention can be more equitably distributed is a distinct question, requiring consideration of the distribution of power and relative social worth. We have seen that allocating attention raises questions not unlike distributing wealth. There is, indeed, a close relation between the distributions of attention and wealth, as both are distributed highly unequally and those privileged in the economic sphere have many advantages in claiming more attention for themselves in daily life. Changes in the amount of attention that different groups receive is dependent on the achievement of greater equality in the larger society.

Ultimately, a humane distribution of attention can develop only in an egalitarian society, in which no group is defined as intrinsically more worthy than any other. While sexual and class inequalities persist, it is possible to identify certain changes that have already begun in America and may contribute to a more humane allocation of attention between men and women and among economic actors.

CHANGING SEX ROLES

Men have traditionally dominated attention because of their monopolization of economic, social, and cultural power. We have seen that males gain attention by virtue of a patriarchal division of roles that assigns the major attention-giving ones to women. In addition, patriarchy creates models of masculine and feminine personality that encourage self-orientation among men and other-orientation among women.

Changes thus depend on the redefinition of male and female roles and identity. The social definition of the female around her biological reproductive roles is the institutional basis for both the other-orientation of women and the self-orientation of men. The development of self-orientation is always linked to a structural responsibility for independent functioning in the economy and society at large—the traditional domain of the male—while other-orientation is tied to familial and child-care roles. The prolonged dependency of children, as well as the needs of infants for continuing special attention, necessitates on the part of the caretaker a transcendence of the egoistic mode; the needs of children are one of the major species considerations which powerfully counteract narcissistic tendencies and create in every society the need for some measure of other-orientation. Since child-care roles are defined in patriarchy as female, this creates constraints only against female narcissism and permits the self-orientation of the male to remain relatively unfettered.

In advanced industrial societies it is the narcissism of the male that has been acutely heightened and most urgently requires the counteracting restraint implicit in child-care roles. The intensive self-orientation of the male can change only if he is socialized to new roles that explicitly demand attentiveness to others. Since male worth is now contingent upon success in economic roles which require extraordinary self-orientation, male egoism is likely to be mitigated only by new expectations for men that involve a decline in pressures for self-directed achievement and a new emphasis on the ability to respond to people. A radical restructuring of the primary attention-giving (i.e., child-care) roles, where men, like women, are expected to develop a capacity to give attention to children, may be the most important element in such a change.

The current trend in America is one in which women are being slowly granted access to the public sphere without major change in the roles played by men in relation to children and the home. The impact of this change on the other-orientation of women is unclear, but no fundamental transformation in male self-orientation is implied. The change in sex roles may indeed be taking a form which only reinforces the general trend in society toward greater self-orientation, that is, one which legitimates for the female the same narcissistic behavior (including attention-getting psychology) as the male, and encourages in neither sex other-orientation or the capacity to give attention. No change in sex roles, in fact, can significantly alter the egoistic, competitive organization of attention as long as economic and social conditions demand self-orientation on the part of one or both sexes. Changes broader than sex-role change are thus required.

SOCIAL CLASS AND SOCIAL CHANGE

The domination of attention by privileged economic groups is inevitable as long as the class structure itself persists. The essential social-psychological meaning of a class system is that one group is defined as "better" than another and thus more entitled to attention. Members of subordinate classes are always placed in a state of uncertainty about their own worth; this undercuts their capacity to assert themselves and claim greater attention.

It is appropriate to conclude with some assessment of the meaning of change in the economic system, not only because it is the only way in which the class-based inequalities can be reduced, but also because the economic system is such an important factor contributing to individualism. The economic imperative of self-interested behavior and the reigning institutions of private property and profit all enhance and intensify the individual's focus on himself. In social orders where economic institutions encourage cooperative rather than egoistic and competitive behavior, an economic basis for other-orientation is established; thus, the experience of Japan suggests that a more communitarian economic system limits the development of excessive individualism in the society at large and introduces strong constraints on the intensified self-orientation that plagues most Western societies.

We have seen that individualism is deeply rooted in American culture; even major changes in the economic order are not likely to completely erode the individualism entrenched in the American cultural tradition. Under conditions of greater economic security and reduced economic competition, however, individualism in American society may diminish, permitting greater concern with others. People might remain individualistic in many respects, yet become less egoistic and more capable of giving attention. This suggests at least the possibility of a less narcissistic social character and more humane social relations in which people share attention and become responsive to each other's needs.

Conclusion to the Second Edition

The pursuit of attention is eternal. Ramses II, the great Egyptian pharoah, built pyramids to ensure that he would be remembered for thousands of years after his death. Nero, the infamous Roman emperor, built a 120-foot-high sculpture of his head haloed with solar rays identifying him as the god Apollo. Louis XV of France had 10,000 servants to attend to him day and night. Napoleon blazoned Paris and other cities with thousands of sculpted letters "N" and liked to show off both his remarkable knowledge and beautiful hands.[1]

Lord Chesterfield of England wrote this self-description as a young aristocrat: "I talk a great deal, I am loud and peremptory . . . and above all I spend an immense sum on my hair, powder, and feathers." He later advised against such brazen displays, and many elites throughout history—though they maintained a slave or servant class whose mission was to proffer desired attention—have pursued attention more discreetly. In the great European capitals of the seventeenth and eighteenth centuries, for example, noblemen and -women flocked to intellectual salons like that of Madame Sevigny in Paris and created one of the most refined competitions for attention: parrying their honed wit and poetic skills to charm the cultivated audience. Displays of intellect, of exquisite conversational skill, and of sublime artistic gifts show that the pursuit has never been easy to disentangle from the foibles of human nature nor from the progress of civilization itself.[2]

Commoners throughout history have pursued their own forms of attention. Most European men and women over the last millennium could not afford the extravagant fashions seen in court, but they sought each other's attention by seductively displaying their bodies and dancing skills. Storytellers have always competed for attention in the tavern or marketplace by spinning the most entertaining yarns, and jesters by cracking the most clever jokes. While women and slaves through much of history were denied the right to pursue public attention, men over the centuries have competed for it by seeing who could gamble most boldly, fight most bravely, swear most obscenely, brag most colorfully, perform athletic feats most brilliantly, or drink most outrageously.

This enduring history might suggest that there is nothing new about what we have described in this book—and nothing we can do about it. Every era in history has its own forms of the pursuit of attention, which are driven by enduring passions of sex, power, and ego. But our modern American version of the pursuit is unique, and perhaps uniquely alienating. New conditions of individualism, more advanced than in any earlier period of history, have freed us to pursue uninhibited self-development and happiness that could, paradoxically, doom us to ever more stress and an unhappy pursuit of attention. Since I first wrote this book, these trends are intensifying in a way that I could not have imagined. While I shall describe the deep-rooted causes of our new pursuit here, I will also suggest there are ways that we can change our situation for the better.

I have written earlier of the "overburdened self" that plagues our times. To be overburdened is to feel besieged—whether by an overcrowded schedule and too few hours in the day, by a rash of pressures about money or one's career, or by emotional troubles in marriage or family life. As the burden grows, people become more preoccupied, churning over and over in their minds how to solve work and personal problems. This state of mind breeds a kind of survivalist mentality that permits little focus on others and fuels an obsessive attention on oneself.

In all eras the self has faced challenges, but in modern times, as I argued in the last chapter, we have to cope increasingly on our own. Through most of history, people have been tied all their lives to small communities—extended families, tribes, villages—that limited freedom but gave people the security of knowing that their problems would be shared by the group as a whole. Modern capitalism destroyed such permanent and all-encompassing communities, freeing each of us to take our own path but exposing us also to the cold chill of sinking or swimming alone. Herein, I argued, lie the social roots of today's over-burdened self and the modern pursuit of attention.

C. Wright Mills emphasized that sociology's mission was to show how our private character is shaped by economic and societal systems. My argument has been that the rise of the modern market system creates a "trickle-down" chain of effects on personal life; what trickles down—through mechanisms that I never fully specified—is a set of individualistic codes of competition and self-interest so pervasive that they revolutionize even how we talk and pursue attention. To explain my main argument more clearly, we can identify five links of the chain: 1) *systemic revolution*—the long rise of the capitalistic market out of the graveyard of feudalism shifts economic ownership and initiative toward entrepreneurs, merchants, and corporations without community roots; 2) *cultural transformation*—the new capitalist actors enact and promote a radical new culture of individualism—articulated by intellectuals, teachers, preachers, parents, and politicians—that prizes individual self-interest over community loyalty; 3) *institutional transformation*—corporations structurally weaken community by slowly gaining control over the jobs and capital on which community life depends; 4) *individualization of everyday life*—as communities decline, individuals become more atomized and self-reliant, carrying burdens once borne by communities themselves; 5) *shifts in character and symbolic interaction*—as individual burdens intensify, our ways of relating to one another inevitably change, making us ever more focussed on ourselves (self-oriented characters) and less inclined or able to give attention to others.

When I first made this argument, I failed to realize that the centuries-long process of separation of the individual from the group was far from complete. Twenty years ago our families, neighborhoods, and workplace communities had been weakened but not decimated. Today, we see a more advanced stage of the breakdown of traditional communities, as a revolutionary form of global capitalism breeds a new culture of hyper-individualism. This adds burdens on the already burdened self, fueling self-preoccupation and a new pursuit of attention.

For most of us, hyper-individualism brings freedom but also a kind of "double trouble." Freud wrote that work and love are the only two things that matter in life. He left out a few things but was right that our sense of well-being depends on our feelings of security at work and home. When work and family become unstable and undependable at the same time, the burdens on the self grow and new needs for support and attention come to the fore.

Double trouble—the simultaneous shift toward less secure attachments at work and home—is a sea change rocking our millennial turn; it sits at the center of the chain connecting systemic changes in our economy and culture with the personal insecurity firing up the pursuit of attention. The rise of disposable work reflects a meltdown in the corporate communities that existed when I first wrote this book. The corporate system is birthing a new workforce of temps, part-timers, independent contractors, leased employees, freelancers, and "temporary permanents." The middle class has morphed into the "anxious class."[3]

A colleague once told me a fable about a photographer who was filming people walking among the skyscrapers in Rockefeller Center in New York City. He saw anxiety increasingly contort their faces. The photographer became so fascinated that he used a zoom lens to focus in on their faces, desperately trying to understand the cause of their distress by closing in on their expressions. But the photographer could not discover the problem because his zoom lens prevented him from seeing that all the tall buildings were collapsing.

Just as the photographer needed a wide-angle lens to understand the problem, so we need now to examine the larger social structure to understand our changing character and need for attention. The collapsing buildings for the new anxious class are the destruction of the stable jobs that were once pillars in our lives. As they disintegrate, in the wake of a new economic revolution, we gain certain opportunities but lose the economic security that the middle class took a century to build.

A few years ago, I interviewed about fifty temps and part-timers who illustrate how such large-scale systemic change trickles down. One woman temped in an office of a local university. She told me that to get to her assigned workspace, she had to walk past a long column of permanent employees. In her first several weeks, nobody ever looked up and met her eyes. This subtle shift in civil attention patterns turned her into an invisible person and fed the insecurity that sticks like glue to the disposable worker.[4]

Attention denial is only one of the many occupational hazards burdening our new disposable workforce; these added burdens create new types of stress and self-preoccupation that subtly change our social relationships and the way we need or seek attention. In my interviews, I found that most contingent workers are subjected to new and sometimes terrible indignities creating both economic and interpersonal humiliation. One accountant, who had lost his job and so found accounting stints through a temp service for professionals, told me that his financial situation had deteriorated so much that he could not buy clothes for his family or new brakes for his old car. A clerical worker admitted that he felt so marginalized in his changing temp jobs that he typically ate his lunch alone in the parking garage. A Hispanic woman who temped stated that she encountered blatant racial discrimination and sexual harrassment that the employers in her previous permanent job would never dare do. Several temps expressed that they could not think about getting into relationships now. They were too preoccupied to deal with the demands of intimate relations; their unpredictable schedules didn't permit settling into a domestic life; many couldn't securely support themselves, let alone anyone else. One freelancer said that the only kind of long-term relation she could even imagine at this point would be with her cat.

These may seem extreme cases. Most Americans still enter relationships and build families. But the temp experience shows how changes in economic institutions can transform people's fundamental sense of worth or respect. As they get less attention—or a more demeaning form of it—in the new job environment, their sense of being devalued becomes a daily, sometimes obsessive psychological burden, and they describe themselves as so preoccupied that they have nothing to give others.

As corporate loyalty becomes an oxymoron, even the most secure workers know that as they get older, they may be downsized and replaced by younger and cheaper recruits. Job insecurity spreading through the whole workforce slowly changes the quality of self-absorption and social relationships. As people learn that corporations are no longer going to take care of them, they of necessity focus more on their own careers and, in situations of outsourcing and downsizing, are increasingly bent on saving their own skins.

What I call "job genocide"—the end of the permanent jobs that built our middle class—increases economic stress, raises the general sense of insecurity, and forces everyone to focus more on themselves to survive and get ahead. As one temp stated, "the only person I can really pay attention to right now is me." That's a sentiment that increasingly fits the whole workforce with most of us having to work harder to succeed. As people become preoccupied with hanging on to disappearing jobs or to getting ahead in a competitive environment that demands more and more of their attention, the ability to give attention to others inevitably erodes.[5]

The end of the permanent job is the first part of double trouble; the second is the destabilization of marriage and the growing contingency of all personal relationships. Secure marriages are the second foundation on which we have built our lives, but we increasingly live in an era of both temporary jobs and impermanent marriages. Divorce in the United States is higher than in almost any other country and remains much higher than it historically has been here. More than 50 percent of marriages break up, as do 67 percent of second marriages and 75 percent of third marriages. As our ties to our companies have become "loose connections," so too have our most intimate bonds.[6]

The increasing acceptability of divorce may be liberating, but it raises anxiety and burdens on the self. Just as all workers feel less secure as millions of new jobs become disposable, so people whose marriages seem stable may feel apprehensive in an age of serial monogamy. As we trust a bit less in the future of our relationships, we tend to become more self-protective and more self-interested, realizing that the only person who may be looking out for "me" in the end is me.[7]

This changes the quality of relationships and inevitably affects patterns of giving and getting attention both inside and outside marriage. Giving attention requires emotional generosity or at least availability, which is still present in most marriages but particularly vulnerable to the stresses of double trouble. If you are worried about your job, it is harder to listen to your spouse's problems. If you are worried about your marriage, it may also be harder to listen to his or her own troubles, if only because your anxiety increases your self-absorption and makes it harder to give attention to anyone but yourself.

I talked some years ago to a college student who was paying her way through college by moonlighting as a call girl. She said that she was amazed that the men who patronized her often did not want sex but simply somebody to talk to. Most felt that their wives did not have the time or patience to listen—and many seemed to need nothing more than a person who would give them sympathetic attention.

This is an old story that prostitutes tell, but it may be a sign of our times that so many new institutions have grown up to give spouse-like attention. One is our new therapeutic culture, in which people pay high sums to psychotherapists for emotionally sensitive attention that makes them feel worthwhile. Another is the cadre of secretaries and administrative assistants whose most important job is to provide their bosses with attention that working, negligent, or divorced spouses no longer offer. Yet another is the horde of new service workers who deliver us everything from our groceries or cooked meals to round-the-clock child care. We are moving toward a service economy that delivers personal attention as its main product.

The collapse of our stable marriages combined with the fall of our stable jobs rock the earth. Many of us feel buffered from one or both changes, but as they spread together through society they catalyze the trickle down that ultimately fuels our pursuit of attention. This chain has all the complicated links noted earlier, but the most critical is the increased individualization of values—caused by the new institutions of temporary workplaces and families that place our growing stressful burdens on our own shoulders. Thereby our hunger for support and attention is increased and our ability to give eroded.

Powerful forces in the economy and culture give rise to double trouble. Ultimately, such trouble reflects the triumph of the marketplace, which gives its blessing to no relationships beyond those profitable at the moment. Corporations—which only thirty years ago stood up for a moral covenant with workers—have increasingly embraced the naked market ethos, shedding long-term workers like flies and disavowing obligations to workers and communities alike. Meanwhile, the market ethos is spreading rapidly into private life as well, infecting ordinary social relations with the new "me, me, me" mentality of the Seinfeld generation that breeds both dysfunctional short-term relationships and a more comically robust form of conversational narcissism.

It remains speculative just how deeply double trouble will reshape how we relate and give attention to each other, if only because it is such a historically novel phenomenon. At the first writing of this book, double trouble had not yet emerged on the landscape. Now it is well entrenched but so new that we do not yet have conclusive evidence of how it is remaking our social lives. New research into the pursuit of attention in the coming century will help tell us how we are changing and coping.

A few years ago, my closest friend of a quarter century—who was a generation older than I—learned that he had a serious disease and would die soon. Many people in this situation withdraw from social life and friendships. Others drain their family and friends by virtue of the support and attention they soak up. My friend did neither.

As death drew nearer, my friend radiated a beautiful new life energy. Rather than withdrawing, he gathered a growing community of people around him. Rather than draining others, he gave unstintingly of himself to the growing numbers of old and new friends who wanted to be close to him, even as he also sparkled with the shine of the loving attention that people were so eager to shower upon him. With me, as he always had, he listened to my pedestrian problems, when his were far more grave. In our final conversation only hours before he lost consciousness, he was more focussed on me than on himself.

My friend's name was Morrie—and he became famous after publication of the best-selling book, *Tuesdays with Morrie*. I dedicated the first edition of *The Pursuit of Attention* to Morrie, who taught me that there is nothing more human than the simple act of giving attention to another. In my eulogy at his memorial service, I said this: "Morrie gave the supreme gift of presence. He was with you without reserve. When you talked to Morrie, you knew that he saw you and wanted you and cared about you. Just you. You were, for a moment, the most important person in the world."[8]

All his life Morrie had studied the philosopher Martin Buber, and he believed that the highest human aspiration was to achieve an "I-Thou" form of communication, in which the pursuit of attention yields to a sacred open-hearted dialogue. Morrie, whose capacity to listen with loving attention seemed inexhaustible, believed that we could all transcend our culturally conditioned narcissism—and he was living proof of the possibility. But in an interview with Ted Koppel when Morrie was close to death, he rasped "ego, ego, ego—all is ego." He was not naive about the difficulties—he knew that revolutionary cultural transformation would take centuries—but he believed that we could change. Morrie had worked hard on himself all his life to enhance his self-awareness and nurture his open heart, and he had to make difficult decisions that face many Americans, such as sacrificing time he needed for his career to nurture his kids and friends. He believed that others could move beyond "me, me, me," but he realized that this required not just personal change but transformation of our economy and larger culture.[9]

Here lies the secret of change: recognizing that we can only change ourselves with others as we rebuild community and create a less self-oriented market system. In our extreme individualistic culture, the only change we are coming to believe in is personal. But if we do not build more cooperation and more human values into our economy and society, all our personal efforts to become more loving human beings—a goal that Morrie now symbolizes for so many Americans—will come to little.

If I am right that the pursuit of attention is rooted in our excessive individualism, which is itself rooted largely in the triumph of the market, then a big agenda of change lies in front of us. C. Wright Mills told us that as we probe deeper into our most important personal problems, we realize that they nearly always reflect public issues which require social and political change. Our habits of the heart are shaped by social institutions. This means that while we have to take responsibility to change our own behavior—for nobody can do that for us—we also cannot and must not shun responsibility for larger social change.[10]

Personal change remains a key part of the struggle for societal change. Even sociologists have to acknowledge that biological temperament plays a role in the ways we pursue attention. Our personalities, heavily shaped both by temperament and parental upbringing, are obviously one prime factor in the pursuit. The self-oriented or narcissistic character may be seeking to compensate for tormenting deficits in parental love and attention that can take a lifetime to heal.

We have seen that the pursuit, with its roots in our economy and culture, cannot be reduced to clinical abnormality. But undoubtedly many of the most avid participants are individuals whose excessive needs for attention are rooted in a history of neglect, abuse, or less traumatic forms of childhood hurt that are widespread in American families. Years of often painful emotional work are required to change oneself, but the rewards of even small progress may include greater self-respect and the capacity to sustain a loving relationship.

A huge industry of personal and spiritual change has grown to help people change themselves. Psychotherapy and group counseling of all forms, as noted earlier, have spread partly because there are so many people now prepared both to sell and pay for attention. Although it is a big business, personal or drug-based therapy is sometimes a powerful instrument of personal change; it can breed self-awareness and help narcissistic individuals understand and restrain their tendencies to call attention to themselves.

Group training in schools and businesses now teaches interpersonal skills, including how to listen and give real attention before talking. Support and self-help groups often employ awareness techniques to make people conscious of hogging the floor and to ensure that everyone gets air time; some insist that everyone speak before a prior speaker gets a second turn. Spiritual groups and religious institutions teach prayer, meditation, and moral rules that can help people curb their ego, and it is true that if everyone observed the Golden Rule in ordinary talk, conversational narcissism might become a relic. I have seen all these approaches work, and although they do not change narcissists into saints, they offer insights and emotional skills that aid people's growth over time. The kind of change we are talking about demands deep changes in individuals, and we should build into our families, schools, and workplaces far more resources and time for people to develop their capacity for self-reflection and personal change. But as I argued in the first edition, much of our new culture of personal change actually fuels individualism by propagating the view that we can change ourselves without changing society—or worse, that the only thing we ever need to change is ourselves.

If the pursuit of attention is the spoiled fruit of uninhibited individualism, then the social change we need is clear: new and stronger forms of community and community-based values. At the end of the first edition, I argued that if individualism was to grow out of control like a cancer in the United States, spontaneous movements might arise to help people create new forms of community in their lives and to promote solidarity and social justice. Although they are small and fragmented, and though they could be crushed by antagonists or sputter out from lack of money or recruits, such movements have now begun to emerge and they are a potential counter-weight to market-based values of "me first."[11]

A new kind of public conversation and activism is now rising in the United States to revitalize "civil society"—the nonprofit institutions of family, neighborhood, and voluntary groups of all kinds that serve the community. There is now much conversation among both liberals and conservatives about how to strengthen the family and help parents give more loving attention to their children. Since how we pursue attention is profoundly shaped by the quality and amount of attention our parents give us as kids, the effort to support parents is of great importance.

Civil society activists are rightly focussed on the needs and character of children. The rise of a new generation of latchkey kids, who have nobody to see them off in the morning or at home to greet them after school, bodes badly for the future. A generation of young people deprived of parental attention will compensate with an exaggerated pursuit throughout their lives. Civil society depends on a robust set of policies—from head start and health care, to medical leave and parental sabbaticals, to better wages and benefits—that are essential for parents to be present and give children the necessary attention.

Neighborhood groups all over the country have also sprung up to build affordable housing, clean up the streets, and advocate for jobs, and more and more of them now see their most important mission as building community. Thousands of charities and service organizations on and off campus are offering economic assistance and personal attention to people who need it, and labor and human rights groups are sprouting everywhere to advocate more respect and resources for dispossessed or stigmatized social groups. The new success of labor unions in organizing contingent workers—such as the part-time workers at UPS or the immigrant workers in textile sweatshops—has great significance, since unions will have to be at the forefront of any movement to restore security and dignity to the workforce.[12]

Most of these groups seem less than revolutionary, but they challenge the prevailing individualism. Many groups are trying mainly to help themselves, but they also have a clear passion for giving to others and building community. Underlying this emerging community-oriented movement is the simple idea of civility as a foundation for coming together. The most elementary kind of civility is civil attention: the need and right that we all have to be seen, valued, and given respectful attention as members of the community.

The biggest failure of these community-oriented movements

is the inability to unite and challenge the principles of the "free market." This is a serious problem and one rooted partly in a lack of understanding. Most community-based grass roots groups, as well as the most influential communitarian thinkers, have yet to see that capitalism is both a builder and a great destroyer of character and social relationships and that the fundamental tension of our age is between the market and the community.[13]

Markets have many virtues, among them the production of modern prosperity. Since affluence vastly reduces the harsh stresses of survival that preoccupied preindustrial peoples, markets create a foundation for more humane and generous social relations. While markets bring competition, they also breed forms of freedom and security that can civilize daily life and humanize the pursuit of attention. But when markets grow too large or powerful, they can slowly infect a whole society with a lethal competitiveness and egoism. The unrestrained markets of our global economy, while they spread capital and technology, also spread greed and selfishness—and have now become a threat throughout the world to community and to the values of democracy and solidarity essential to a more civil pursuit.[14]

The prairie revolt against global companies such as Wal-Mart coming into communities and destroying local business, or the populist anger that erupts when GM closes a plant in Michigan and exports the local jobs to Mexico, reflects a visceral awareness of the tension today between multinational corporations and local communities. Markets seek the cheapest costs and the greatest profits anywhere on the planet, and when companies downsize or outsource, they wreak financial and psychological havoc on the world's workers and communities. Markets treat these vast social costs as "externalities" to which they are blind and indifferent. Among the costs are subtle ones that inflame the pursuit: changes in our self-esteem and emotional availability to one another as we struggle to survive in more short-term and stressful jobs and relationships.

Since I wrote the first edition, the problem has grown larger. As markets and corporations have globalized rapidly in the last two decades, they have been systematically cutting their ties to community, including that of the nation itself. Global companies now play one community or one nation off against the other as a core competitive policy, seeking to cheapen costs further by forcing communities to lower their standards in a global race to the bottom. Indifference to the community has been replaced all too often by a calculated strategy that subverts it, weakening our sense that there is anyone but ourselves left to support us.

The ideology of "free markets" has become more powerful and fevered. Markets have always championed self-interest, but economists since Adam Smith have historically recognized that the trust and solidarity that communities breed are essential to the success of markets themselves. After all, one cannot buy and sell on the market without a measure of trust and sympathy between buyer and seller or employer and worker. Today, global financial markets and companies view loyalty to employees and communities as a burden that undermines efficiency. Hence, the creation of the disposable workforce and the virus-like spread of economic and psychological insecurity that fuels the pursuit of attention.[15]

Surprisingly, then, the most important social change that we need to make to humanize our daily interactions is in our current religion of the market. We have to decide finally that people are more important than profits and that there are basic community standards and human rights which corporations all over the world must respect. This will require that we give communities and the workers that live in them a seat at the table with investors in corporate board rooms and global financial institutions—and that these institutions focus intently on the needs of the world's employees to be secure and valued as human beings. It will also require getting money out of politics so that leaders can once again serve the community rather than the rich.[16]

While community-based organizations and labor unions will have to come together to bring such change, corporations themselves may play a surprisingly constructive role. The rise of a corporate social responsibility movement among business leaders is a sign that free market radicalism subverts the corporation itself. Corporations want cheap labor but also motivated and loyal workers, and they are discovering that when workers feel devalued and go out only for themselves, the company courts disaster. Thus, as corporations embrace the rhetoric of teamwork, participation, and empowerment, they are—in a spirit quite contradictory to their passion for disposable workers—beginning to think again of themselves as communities. Corporations depend intensely on not only the technical but also the social and emotional skills of their employees. In a new economy that gave companies the right incentives, they could become a significant institution in the human development of the labor force, just as unions have to play a major role in building solidarity and creating a culture in which people pay attention to and care more for one another.[17]

Many historians believe that societies move in cycles. We have probably not seen the peak of market-based individualism that has been gathering steam for most of this millennium. But it may be that in the new millennium, the human costs will mount so steeply that a transformative shift will push us toward a new vision of community and cooperation. Markets will not disappear, and we can be certain that self-interest will continue to play a leading role in human affairs. We can be sure as well that the pursuit of attention will remain an eternal source of fascination, occupying our descendants for centuries to come. But we can hope that our new pursuit will alienate us less and humanize us more, even as we recognize that as long as we engage in the dance of social life, the pursuit of attention will always be with us.

Notes

Introduction to the Second Edition

1. For a provocative discussion of celebrity and everyday life, see Neal Gabler, *Life the Movie: How Entertainment Conquered Reality*. NY: Knopf, 1998. For another recent discussion of the banalization of fame and celebrity, which helps turn many people toward their own variety of the pursuit of attention, see Michael Kimmelman, "How Photography Makes Celebrity So Irresistible," *The New York Times*, July 9, 1999, pp. B29, 31. See also Leo Braudy, *The Frenzy of Renown: Fame and Its History*. NY: Vintage, 1997. Also P. David Marshall, *Celebrity and Power: Fame in Contemporary Culture*. Minneapolis: University of Minnesota Press, 1997.
2. Kathy Lee Peiss, *Hope in a Jar: The Making of America's Beauty Culture*. NY: Metropolitan Books, 1998.
3. Sharlene Hesse-Biber, *Am I Thin Enough Yet? The Cult of Thinness and the Commercialization of Identity*. NY: Oxford University Press, 1997.
4. For a historical perspective on cosmetic surgery and related phenomena, see Elizabeth Haiken, *Venus Envy: A History of Cosmetic Surgery*. Baltimore: Johns Hopkins Press, 1997. A spate of books on body-building and male fashion testifies to men's new obsession with physical display. See, for example, Robert Wolff, *Body-Building 101: Everything You Need to Know to Get the Body You Want*. NY: Contemporary Books, 1999.
5. Wally Lamb, *I Know This Much Is True*. NY: Regan, 1999. Caroline Knapp, *Drinking: A Love Story*. NY: Dial, 1996.
6. Nancy Day, *Sensational TV: Trash or Journalism?* NY: Enslow Publishers, 1996.
7. Christopher Lasch, *The Culture of Narcissism*. NY: Basic Books; revised, NY: Norton, 1991. On Conversational Narcissism, see A. Knapp Vangelisti and J. Daly "Conversational Narcissism," *Communication Monographs*, 57 (1990). For a review of the academic literature, see also Terri L. Kelly, "Literature Review: Conversational Narcissism in Hyperpersonal Interaction," posted on the Internet at http://odin.cc.pdx.edu/~psu17799/sp511.htm.
8. David Riesman, *The Lonely Crowd: A Study of the Changing American Character*. New Haven, Conn.: Yale University Press, 1969.
9. Nathan Cobb, "Big Cam on Campus," *The Boston Globe*, March 10, 1999, pp. A1, 17.
10. Jennifer Mendelsohn, "Publicity Hounds," In-flight *Delta Airlines Magazine*, Spring, 1999, pp. 55–7.

11. Claudia H. Deutsch, "A Hands-on-the-Helm Leader," *New York Times*, June 13, 1999, p. 2 of business section.
12. For a sociological analysis of credit cards and contemporary consumerism, see George Ritzer, *Expressing America: A Critique of the Global Credit Card Society*. Chicago: Pine Forge Press, 1995.
13. Thorstein Veblen, *The Theory of the Leisure Class*. NY: Penguin Classics, 1994.
14. Jennifer Mendelsohn, "Publicity Hounds," op.cit., pp. 55, 57.

Part I Introduction

1. "Informal" interactions can be distinguished from "formal" interactions, which are those strictly organized according to institutionally defined roles and tasks, as in classrooms or psychotherapy, for example. Since people are not free of status expectations in informal conversation, "formal" behavior occurs in informal interactions. Similarly, while informal behavior occurs mainly in informal interactions, it takes place also in formal ones.
2. Hans Gerth and C. Wright Mills, *Character and Social Structure*, p. 8. [Complete details of publication for all references are given in the Bibliography.]
3. Fromm's most important works in this regard are his earlier ones: *Escape From Freedom* and *The Sane Society*.
4. See p. 10.
5. To insure the "naturalness" of the interactions, those observed were not told of the study nor informed that they were being observed. Strict confidentiality of the observational reports was maintained and the identity of those observed, when known to the observer, was not recorded on the report. Observation focused on the attention-dynamics and only indirectly on the content of what was being said. The reports do not include detailed accounts of the substance of the conversation; they do include notes on how long, and by what process, each person held the focus of attention, but are only schematic in regard to the specific development of topics.
6. Volunteers were drawn from students, faculty, and nonprofessional white-collar and blue-collar employees from three university communities in the Boston area. The volunteers were informed that the study was concerned with aspects of ordinary social interaction, but were not told specifically of the focus on attention. After their conversation was completed, they were fully informed of the nature and purpose of the study.

Chapter 1

1. John Bowlby, *Maternal Care and Mental Health*. René Spitz, "Anaclitic Depression," in *Psychoanalytic Study of the Child*.
2. R. D. Laing, *The Divided Self*.
3. No position is taken here regarding a theory of psychological needs or the status of

attention as an elementary psychological requirement. Psychological theories are vague regarding the social and biological origins of needs and are not easily reconciled with the finding that what constitutes "satisfaction" of a need appears to vary significantly in different cultures. Whether a need for attention exists among adults in all cultures is not a central concern here. The focus is rather on the social factors governing how attention is exchanged and distributed in everyday life.

4. Erving Goffman, *Behavior in Public Places*, p. 24.

5. Unfocused interactions take place in public settings such as subway cars and waiting rooms where strangers are physically together but are not conversing. Goffman (*Behavior in Public Places*, Chapter 2) also identifies a third kind of interaction which he calls "partly focused." This involves situations in which certain participants are talking while others are present but formally excluded from the right to take part. An example is the interaction in a restaurant in which the waiter is expected to keep an eye on his customers but not to take part in their conversation. Aspects of the allocation of attention in "unfocused" and "partly focused" interactions are given some consideration in the second part of this book. Throughout, however, the main concern is with the dynamics of focused interaction.

6. The definitions of the visual and cognitive focus require further explication. In all verbal interaction, the common visual focus at any given moment is occupied by the person talking. Over the course of an entire interaction, the person who speaks the most receives the most "visual" attention. However, the identification of talking with visual attention has certain limitations, particularly in two-person interactions, as each person looks at the other and not at a common object. Thus it is not possible to speak of a visual focus. To say that the person talking is the person receiving visual focus is an extension from three or more person interaction, where a common visual focus does exist and is normally centered on the person speaking.

The term cognitive attention derives from the condition of being at the center of others' cognition or thought. In conversation, a person receives "cognitive" focus whenever the topic is focused on himself or herself. Most ordinary conversation is about one or another of the conversationalists. The allocation of cognitive attention thus concerns who will become the predominant subject or topic of the conversation. If the focus is on some abstract topic or on a person not present, then none of the conversationalists involved receives cognitive focus.

While my concern is primarily with verbal interaction, it should be pointed out that cognitive and visual attention can also be exchanged in nonverbal interaction. When lovers look into each other's eyes without speaking, they are exchanging visual attention. The cognitive focus in nonverbal interaction is the person who is the subject or center of both persons' awareness (that is, the person being thought about by both persons). Thus, in mother-infant interaction, the child receives predominant cognitive focus as the awareness of both is centered on him. In conversation, the cognitive focus is the person being talked about; in nonverbal interaction, it is the one being thought about or the common object of mental awareness.

7. The discussion of allocation in formal interaction is reserved for Part II, beginning on pp. 33 ff.

8. The concept of individualism has been used not only to characterize cultural systems,

but economic systems, philosophical and political traditions, and psychological dispositions. It is thus associated with a wide range of meanings in different contexts. These include the idea of "egoism" in philosophical and psychological thinking, the freedom of the individual in political individualism, and laissez faire and individual initiative in economic behavior. Of special interest here are forms of cultural and social individualism that define patterns of responsibility and concern for self and others. The emphasis on principles of individual responsibility and self-interest underlie most forms of individualism. Because of the nature of the subject matter, I am also centrally concerned with social psychological expressions of individualism that reflect "self-orientation" or a primary concern with the self (egoism). This is elaborated in the second chapter. For a brief review of the different meanings of individualism, see Steven Lukes, *Individualism*.

9. The dominant culture of individualism in American society has its roots in economic, religious, and social conditions. Most observers have stressed the relation of American individualism to American capitalism and the ways in which economic individualism breeds individualistic social ideology and cultural patterns. Others have stressed the importance of the Protestant cultural heritage as well as the special patterns of mobility, transcience, and isolation from established community that characterized frontier life. Following Erich Fromm, I have regarded economic individualism as of special importance and have developed certain parallels between economic and social and psychological modes of individualism. See Erich Fromm, *Escape From Freedom*.

10. I discuss the ritual restraints of the civil order in Chapter 2 on pp. 19 ff. The "freedom" in informal interaction contrasts with the regimentation in formal interaction. In formal settings, such as the classroom, people are expected to take a prescribed amount of initiative consistent with their institutional role. While there is much greater discretion in informal interaction, the freedom is not absolute. Differences in status create different expectations of behavior, with those of higher status normally freer to take more initiatives on their own behalf. The "free initiative" in informal interaction is thus only relative; the limitations associated with status differences are discussed in Part II, where I discuss these "formal" aspects of behavior in informal interactions.

11. Success here means actual effectiveness in gaining or holding attention when one seeks to do so. It should be noted that an individual can receive attention without taking any initiative, as when another conversationalist introduces topics about him or persists in directing attention to him by asking repeated questions. The fundamental characteristic of the individual initiative system is not that it excludes such attention-giving behavior from others but (a) that it places people under minimal and purely ritualized obligations to *initiate* this behavior and (b) that it gives no one the right to expect any attention other than that which comes through his or her own initiative.

12. The essential individualism of the system is effectively masked by the civil norms that demand that people maintain an appearance of interest in and concern for others. Tensions exist between the rituals of sociability and the underlying individualistic imperatives of the attention-system. The ritual system is explored at some length in the next chapter.

13. In ninety percent of the conversations, at least two-thirds of the topics focusing on one of the participants are initiated by that person. From the study of dinner conversations described on p. 7.

14. These observations are drawn from the study of dinner conversations described on p. 7.

15. Obligations regarding responsiveness entail not only a demonstration that one is listening, but a minimal measure of supportive behavior that indicates some interest or at least a willingness to acknowledge the topic of the other. One must distinguish between these required civil responses, which give the speaker the freedom to continue his or her initiatives without blatant interruptions and discretionary efforts by the listener to support the topic of the speaker beyond ritual acknowledgments that he or she is paying attention. Subtle differences in responsiveness significantly affect the extent to which a topic is kept alive. The civil obligations regarding responsiveness indicate that the responsibility for sustaining topics on the floor is not entirely individualized, although it lies predominantly with the initiator.

16. This does not imply that all people constantly compete for attention. While people do frequently compete, many do not either because they do not desire attention in a particular interaction or because they prefer to take initiative only when it is clear that others are not seeking attention themselves. The attitude of the individual must be distinguished from the structure of the allocation system. An analogy can be made with a competitive sport or game in which the players are in a competitive position with one another, but the individual players may be either highly competitive or relatively competitive, or not at all competitive.

17. While attention is not intrinsically "scarce," it tends to become so under the individualistic conditions of allocation and distribution described here. The individualistic attention-norms sanction self-oriented behavior and legitimate efforts to focus attention on oneself. When this becomes the prevailing pattern—and characterizes many of the participants in normal interactions—attention becomes scarce in ordinary conversation, as each person seeks a predominant share of the attention for himself. This theme is analyzed in depth in the next chapter.

18. From the Attention-Interaction Project supervised by the author. See p. 6.

19. Conversely, other personality characteristics are extremely important in gaining attention. The qualities cited most often by observers in the attention-interaction study as characteristic of those winning attention include assertiveness, aggressiveness, animatedness, self-confidence, authoritativeness, and humor. While these qualities are effective in the gaining of attention under conditions of individualism, they are not necessarily more compelling in all cultures. The specific norms of attention-behavior, as well as the particular personality qualities prized in each culture, may lead to different kinds of personalities winning attention in different societies.

20. From the Attention-Interaction Project. Not only was invisibility a common occurrence, but domination of attention by one of the particpants was observed in a majority of the conversations. In three-fourths of the conversations a significant inequality in the distribution of attention was reported, with one person described as clearly dominant in over fifty percent of the conversations.

21. In special interactional settings, such as therapy groups, the dynamics of the inter-

action are themselves a legitimate subject of conversation and it becomes easier for those getting no attention to raise this as a problem for the consideration of the others involved. It is not unusual for members of therapy or counseling groups to complain of not being sufficiently appreciated or noticed. Philip Slater, in personal communication, suggested that the issue of their own invisibility is the most common way that invisible persons in such settings may be able to get any attention. In ordinary conversation, however, awareness of the interactional dynamics of the conversation itself normally remains covert and is introduced explicitly into the conversation only if the ritual order has been blatantly violated or the relationship of those involved has been specifically defined to encompass open consideration of these matters.

Chapter 2

1. In contrast, an "attention-giving" psychology is based on the tendency for the individual to focus attention on the needs and concerns of others as well as himself in social life. While the attention-getting psychology is more consistent with the individualistic norms of the dominant culture and is more pervasive in the society, the attention-giving psychology is expected of members of subordinate groups, especially women, and tends to characterize their behavior in face-to-face interactions with those more powerful.

   While a dominant psychology of attention develops in every culture, there is thus significant variation by sex and social status. I am concerned in this chapter only with the dominant form in American culture. In the second part of the book I examine the variations among groups who occupy different positions in the social structure.

2. In his classic work, *Escape From Freedom*, Fromm discussed the concept of social character and emphasized the primacy of individualism in shaping character structure in modern capitalist cultures. The theme of egoism has been central in many analyses of the psychology bred by individualism. In his work on suicide, Durkheim treated egoism as a response to the weakening of social bonds and traditional collectivities. The disaffiliated individual is centrally self-oriented as his isolation breeds self-absorption and his individualized social and economic position erodes collective purposes and engenders preoccupation with his own needs.

   Several American social theorists have pointed to the emergence of self-orientation as a central element in American social character. Philip Reiff has discussed "psychological man"—a character type bred by modern individualism and concerned primarily with his own personal growth and gratification. Richard Sennett has discussed the fall of "public man" and the rise of the more self-oriented and private man of contemporary culture. Christopher Lasch has spoken of the growth of the narcissistic character as a response to the survival pressures of contemporary individualism. The breakdown of family life and other community supports and the burdening of each individual with economic and social responsibilities formerly shared with others necessarily generates a focus on oneself and preoccupation with one's own needs. These themes are elaborated in the last chapter. See Émile Durkheim, *Suicide*; Philip Reiff, *The Triumph of the Therapeutic*; Richard Sennett, *The Fall of Public Man*; Christopher Lasch, *The Culture of Narcissism*.

3. See Emily Post, *Etiquette*, Chapter 1.

4. These studies are described in the Introduction, pp. 6–7.

5. The ritual order has been richly described by Erving Goffman, "Face-Work," in *Interaction Ritual*.

6. This unawareness may extend to the self-oriented individual himself. Conversational narcissism is typically not conscious behavior but reflects rather a habitual focus on or absorption with oneself that is non-self-consciously expressed in conversational patterns. Use of terminology such as conversational initiatives or strategies should thus not be understood as always referring to willful or manipulative behavior but to unreflective behavior that has the effect of creating shifts in topic and attention.

7. The illustrations of shift-responses here are drawn from the transcriptions of the dinner conversations (see p. 7). The support-responses here are hypothetical, presented in this format to highlight the contrast with shift-responses. Unless otherwise indicated, all examples presented in the text in this chapter are drawn from the transcripts. For purposes of readability, the presentation of the transcripts is nontechnical and does not include special markings denoting pauses or interruptions.

8. Under special circumstances, a support-response can be used as an attention-getting initiative by subtly redirecting the conversation. By asking a certain form of question about the other, for example, the respondent may steer the talk toward new ideas, leading eventually toward a focus on himself. However, it cannot lead to a shift in the next turn in the conversation, and normally sustains the talk on the other's topic for at least several successive turns.

9. That the shift-response is, in fact, often intended as a sharing-response and not as a vehicle to shift topics renders this more plausible. The distinction between the shift-response as a sharing response and as an attention-getting initiative is considered in the following pages. It can be pointed out here that when used for narcissistic purposes of topical initiative, it has attributes of what Reusch has called a tangential response, a speech act which gives the impression of being responsive but does not actually affirm or validate what the other has just said. See Reusch, "The Tangential Response," in Hoch and Zubin (eds.), *Psychopathology of Communication*.

10. There may be certain topics where it is legitimate to introduce oneself into the conversation immediately (for example, to provide certain necessary information for the further unfolding of the topic). The openness in the unfolding of topics and the looseness in the rules regarding the phase at which it is legitimate to introduce the self as subject in talk about others' topics creates the possibility for the exploitation of the shift-response for narcissistic ends.

11. See p. 13.

12. All support-responses are attention-giving responses which allow another conversationalist to hold the topical focus. I have characterized the "strength" of these responses in terms of how active a form of attention they suggest in the listener and how much support they provide for the other to remain as the focus of attention.

13. The absence of all such support-responses entitles the offended party to either inquire directly as to whether the other is listening or to directly express annoyance at the inattentiveness and to expect an apology.

14. See especially Don H. Zimmerman and Candace West, "Sex-Roles, Interruptions and Silences in Conversation," in Barrie Thorne and Nancy Henley (eds.), *Language and Sex.*

15. This leads to one of the most common deceptive practices in conversation, with the respondents mumbling "yeah," "uh huh," or other affirmations while paying only minimal attention and impatiently waiting to introduce their own concerns into the talk.

16. *Relative* discretion is permitted in frequency of use; conversationalists vary in the frequency with which they make background acknowledgments, both because of differences in personality and interactional style and in their characteristic responsiveness. It is worth noting that certain conversationalists who have strong need for validation may find their topics undermined not only by narcissistic others who extend relatively infrequent acknowledgments, but also others who may be responsive but whose conversational style does not involve frequent responses of this kind. Speakers who differ significantly in their use of background acknowledgments or other support-responses may find it difficult to talk to one another, not understanding the forms of validation which facilitate each other's speech.

17. See Gail Jefferson, "A Case of Precision Timing in Ordinary Conversation: Overlapped Tag-Positioned Address Terms in Closing Sequences," *Semiotica* (1969), pp. 48–96. See also Zimmerman and West, "Sex-Roles."

18. The study by Zimmerman and West, "Sex-Roles," shows a linking of delayed response with premature topic termination and topic changeover, reporting that in at least three of ten transcripts topic closure follows regularly on the heels of a sequence of such repeated delayed responses.

19. Jessie Bernard uses the more general term "minimal response" to refer to what I have called differential use. Her notion of minimal response includes elements of my categories of minimal use as well as differential use. See Bernard, *The Sex Game*, especially Chapter 6.

20. A topic carried by questions is as follows:

MARY: What a day at school.
JOHN: What happened?
MARY: Oh, the kids were just impossible.
JOHN Was it Ann and Larry again?
MARY: Yeah, plus a few others. They were all . . .

Here a comparable topical initiative receives the stronger support-response and is brought to "takeoff" by repetition of supportive questions. The importance of the supportive question in securing the topic of others suggests why narcissistic practice involves a very low reliance on such questions.

Part II Introduction

1. See pp. 2 ff for the definition of informal and formal behavior.

Chapter 3

1. These differences are most pronounced in formal interactions, but emerge in lesser degree in informal interactions as well. In this chapter we look first at formal interactions and then return to consideration of the informal interactions and conversations discussed in Part 1.
2. Patriarchal societies have been defined as those in which economic, political, and cultural authority is exercised primarily by men. For general theoretical discussions of the patriarchal system, see Nancy Chodorow, *The Social Reproduction of Mothering*, and Steven Goldberg, *The Inevitability of Patriarchy*.
3. This is the first of a series of observations of attention-dynamics in everyday social interaction, taken from the Attention-Interaction Project supervised by the author. For a description of the study, see the Introduction, pp. 6–7. All future illustrations, unless otherwise indicated, are drawn from this study.
4. Bernard has stressed the extreme demands of the mother role in American society, including the expectation of self-subordination and accommodation of the attention-demands of the child. She describes the characteristic interactional pattern:

> For perhaps an hour, the woman can maintain a degree of tranquility by centering all of her attention on the child. She tells stories. She plays games. She shares toys. She can meet the child's insatiable demands for attention with moderate ease. As time passes, however, this becomes harder and harder. As she shows signs of flagging, the demands of the child become more and more insistent. In her eagerness to placate the child's demands, she has been rewarding its distressing behavior.

See Jesse Bernard, *The Future of Motherhood*, p. 112–13.
5. Children direct considerable attention to their mothers simply because they are the primary care-takers. This is suggestive of the fact that being in the role of attention-giver is the primary way that women get attention for themselves. Men, in contrast, gain attention without the obligation of assuming attention-giving roles and responsibilities.
6. See Mary Benet, *The Secretarial Ghetto*, p. 72 ff., and Jean Tepperman, *Not Servants, Not Machines: Office-Workers Speak Out*, Chapters 1–2.
7. See Jessie Bernard, *The Future of Marriage*, and Louise Kapp Howe, *Pink Collar Workers*.
8. See especially Robert Bales, *Personality and Social Interaction*, and Robert Bales and Talcott Parsons, *Family, Socialization and Interaction Process*.
9. This research has been reviewed by Jessie Bernard. Based on studies of family inter-

actions and statistics of mental and physical health, Bernard makes a compelling argument that the family provides superior support functions for the husband and is characterized by interactional patterns reflecting male power. See Bernard, *The Future of Marriage.*

10. The importance of the father's status outside the family in shaping attention-dynamics within it is suggested further by this report from an observer of attention-dynamics within his own family:

> My father is undoubtedly the most powerful in this respect. He is a professional with a national reputation and the subtle aura of his authority in the academic world is felt at home. I have always been conscious of the respect he receives from his colleagues and I greatly admire his opinion on everything. The source of his power and attention in the family lies in his credibility. He is always right.

11. From the Attention-Interaction Project. See pp. 6 ff.
12. These roles are examined at length in the next chapter. Some of these roles, such as doctor, carry with them expectations of attention-giving toward clients or patients. It will be shown that many of the attention-giving responsibilities are being removed from the professional's role and delegated to subordinates, who are typically female.
13. The exception is in the exchange of attention with other workers, explored on pp. 69 ff in the next chapter; see also note 25, Chapter 4.
14. See Chapter 2 (pp. 18 ff) for a discussion of the concept of a psychology of attention, including a definition of the "attention-giving" and "attention-getting" psychologies.
15. Mary Rohman, "Conversations: Male and Female Experience" (including transcripts and analysis).
16. Drawn from preliminary interviews by the author of observers selected for the Attention-Interaction Project. In the process of their training, observers were interviewed regarding their own modes of giving and getting attention.
17. From an interview with the author in the Attention-Interaction Project.
18. Philip Slater's work on the relation between narcissism and sexual identity is extremely useful in understanding the psychological characteristics of the self-oriented male. See Slater, "Culture, Sexuality, and Narcissism," in *Footholds: Understanding the Shifting Family and Sexual Tensions in Our Culture.*
19. See Chapter 1 for a review of the individual initiative system.
20. From the Attention-Interaction Project.
21. From the Attention-Interaction Project. These differences have been reported in other studies as well. See in Barrie Thorne and Nancy Henley (eds.), *Language and Sex*, especially the essay by Thorne and Henley, "Difference and Dominance: An Overview of Language, Gender and Society," pp. 5–42.
22. See, for example, Myron Brenton, *The American Male.*
23. This is not to minimize the plight of those less able than most men to live up to the ideal of the masculine personality. Many gentle, unaggressive, or "feminine" men are subject to severe face-to-face punitive treatment, often at the hands of women as well as other men. In winning attention, they are in many respects more disadvantaged

than women because they have less social license to use "feminine" traits, such as emotionality or dependency. Thus, while some of these men hope to receive male privileges of attention, many do not succeed.

24. As indicated earlier (p. 13; see also note 10, Chapter 1), "formal" attention-dynamics play an important part in informal interaction. The different expectations assigned to men and women in informal conversation are the most important example.

25. The principal studies are those by William Soskin and Fred Hilpert, based on observations of male-female conversations in everyday life and in experimental laboratory settings. Both report patterns of greater talkativeness among men. See William Soskin and Vera John, "The Study of Spontaneous Talk," in Roger Barker (ed.) *The Stream of Behavior*, and Fred Hilpert, Cheris Kramer, and Ruth Ann Clark, "Participants' Perceptions of Self and Partner in Mixed-Sex Dyads."

26. See Bernard, "Talk, Conversation, Listening, Silence," in Bernard, *The Sex Game*, Chapter 6, and Rohman, "Conversations."

27. See Barrie Thorne, "Women in the Draft Resistance Movement," p. 268.

28. Ibid.

29. *The New Seventeen Book of Young Living* instructs girls to "concentrate on the other person. Ask questions to draw him out. He'll love talking about himself."

30. See p. 7.

31. See Don Zimmerman and Candace West, "Sex-Roles, Interruptions and Silences in Conversation," in Thorne and Henley (eds.), *Language and Sex*, and Bernard, "Talk, Conversation."

32. This puts in a new perspective on the stereotype of the tongue-wagging woman who talks incessantly, even when no one is listening. Male unresponsiveness means that women must learn to talk with less support or feedback. They must, in a sense, tune out unresponsiveness, either by ignoring it or by becoming invulnerable to it. Otherwise, they will be paralyzed.

33. Males are not only less supportive of female topics but are more aggressive as competitors for their own topics. This suggests that shift-responses (see p. 20) are also sex-linked. Interruptions, for example, a major form of shift-responses, are a male prerogative. Zimmerman and West have shown, in a study of conversations recorded in coffee shops, drug stores, and other public places, that while males frequently interrupt females, the reverse is a relatively rare occurrence. According to the authors, this is linked to a generalized male privilege in abruptly turning talk to his own topics and interests (Zimmerman and West, "Sex-Roles"). My analysis of dinner conversations suggested that while both men and women make abundant use of the shift-response to redirect talk to themselves, males do this more blatantly and display less sensitivity to the needs of women to complete their topics.

34. See Chapter 1 for discussion of this point.

Chapter 4

1. See Richard Sennett and Jonathan Cobb, *The Hidden Injuries of Class*.

2. The working class, as understood here, includes blue-collar and many white-collar

and service workers who are often characterized as "middle class" in popular discourse. The characterization of "middle class" obscures the fact that these workers, many of whom are moderately well paid, do not exercise control over their work or cultural institutions and are subject to the authority of capital and the professional-managerial class. The dominant classes, as understood here, refer to those popularly referred to as the "upper class" and the "upper-middle" class and comprise at most between twenty and thirty percent of the population.

3. Formal interactions are those strictly regulated by institutional roles and purposes. The system for the allocation of attention in formal interactions, based on the organization of attention-getting and attention-giving roles, is described on pp. 35 ff. In the analysis of formal interactions and their relation to class, we are concerned, as indicated earlier, not only with how attention is allocated *within* given interactions, but with the different *access* of members of different groups to formal settings and interactional roles in which they can normally expect attention. We thus explore here both "class" dynamics internal to interactions and the class character of the larger social structure in which attention-getting roles are allocated mainly to privileged groups. For a discussion of this approach, see pp. 36 ff, in the Introduction to Part II.

4. In considering formal interactions in settings such as restaurants, we must distinguish between "focused" and "partly focused" kinds of interactions (pp. 10 ff). "Focused" interaction between waiter and customer occurs whenever they are directly engaged in talk, as when the customer is ordering the food or the waiter inquires how good it tastes. In these interactions, the shared cognitive focus of attention is clearly on the customer, as it is his food, comfort, and needs that are the subject or topic of the interaction and constitute the focus of awareness of both parties in the interaction.

"Partly focused" interaction also occurs between waiter and customer. Goffman has described partly focused interaction as that where there are persons officially present in the situation who are excluded from participation in the interaction. This defines the situation of the waiter at the stage when the meal is being eaten; he is expected to remain discreetly attentive to his customers without taking part in their talk among themselves. Such "partly focused" attention is an important form purchased by customers or clients in other settings as well, for example, from sales personnel in boutiques or department stores or from attending nurses in hospitals. See Erving Goffman, *Behavior in Public Places*, pp. 91 ff.

5. From the Attention-Interaction Project supervised by the author. All examples cited henceforth in this chapter are drawn from this research, unless otherwise specified. This particular report is one of a small number based on participant-observation.

6. An important "privilege" of attention involves the conditions under which the customer can signal those serving him that he wants attention (that is, signal him to engage in direct "focused" interaction). In the ordinary restaurant, as Goffman points out, the waiter, rushed by demands from a number of tables, can pretend not to see the signal of a customer at a given table and thus give himself more time to finish what he is in the process of doing. In the expensive restaurant, where a waiter is

assigned to wait on only one party at a time, the patron is freed from the annoyance of these delays and can expect immediate response to signals for attention.

This is more broadly a problem in the organization of "partly focused" interaction (see p. 10). Waiters are present with the "main participants" (the diners), but are excluded from their "focused" conversation or interaction except when summoned to take part. The condition of summons is linked to the relative status of those involved. The higher the relative status of the "main participants" and the more they are paying for the service, the smaller the cue required to signal and command immediate attention. Summoning others to engage in "focused" interaction is typically a prerogative of status. Those of lower status are expected to be available to such summons while not normally initiating them themselves. Thus, in an illustration mentioned by Goffman, the butler who wishes to engage his master does not normally directly initiate interaction, but may "cough" discreetly to attract his notice. For further discussion of these matters, see Goffman, *Behavior in Public Places*, p. 91 ff.

7. We refer to waiters rather than waitresses here because exclusive restaurants typically employ males to serve and attend to their clientele. This suggests that male attention is deemed more valuable. While attention-giving is expected more regularly of women, the dominant classes have the resources to purchase male attention as a scarce and more prized commodity.

8. An interesting analogy is suggested between the selling of labor power and the selling of attention. In the capitalist market system, both labor and attention are transformed into commodities, with purchase reserved for the dominant classes. The analogy is imperfect in certain ways, as members of the dominant classes, for example, therapists, doctors, lawyers, also sell their attention on the market. They market it, however, for a much higher price and command a much higher return.

9. These roles require the sustaining of the cognitive focus of attention in all role-related interaction on those who employ them. The role is thus comprised of a set of face-to-face interactions, both "focused" and "partly focused," in which the servant surrenders the focus of attention to his master or boss. Since it is not appropriate for the servant, except under special circumstances, to introduce himself or herself as the focus, he or she assumes a role-defined invisibility, discussed further on pp. 69 ff.

Richard Parker indicates that the employment of "domestic help" has declined considerably in the upper class since World War II, with only one in five households employing regular help. Nonetheless, Gabriel Kolko has pointed out that 2.5 million butlers, maids, chauffeurs, and cooks are still employed in private households, predominantly from the upper class. See Richard Parker, *The Myth of the Middle Class*, p. 125, and Gabriel Kolko, *Wealth and Power in America*.

10. Consumption displays bring both "focused" and "unfocused" face-to-face attention. In conversation and other focused interactions, the receptivity of others to an individual's conversational initiatives are significantly affected by his perceived worth. As indicated in the first chapter, external signs of high status play an important role by predisposing others to give credibility to one's statements, to see more humor and sophistication in one's jokes, and, more broadly, to yield the floor and give attention in deference to perceived power or authority. In "unfocused" interactions, where

people are physically together in the same space but are not engaged in talk (as in the subway car or theater), property displays are effective in attracting visual attention. Under circumstances of "conspicuous consumption," as Veblen emphasizes, this is normally associated with unexpressed sentiments of respect, admiration, or envy. See Thorstein Veblen, *The Portable Veblen*, pp. 111 ff.

11. The privileges of class here are defined by standards of taste and elegance. Less privileged women, who adorn themselves with a profusion of gaudy costume jewelry, will command less attention than a privileged woman wearing simple strands of gems encased in precious metals.

12. This is the "unfocused" attention that people receive from strangers with whom they are not directly interacting. Most displays of conspicuous consumption are useful in attracting such "unfocused" attention as well as "focused" attention in conversation. See Chapter 1, pp. 10 ff.

13. The importance of automobiles, and a twist on class privileges, is suggested by a recent advertisement for a dependable compact. A tycoon shown at the wheel, when asked why he chooses this car when he can afford to drive any car he wants, retorts, "I can also afford not to." Those with the most unassailable status thus do not require constant commodity displays.

14. See Stewart Ewen, *Captains of Consciousness*.

15. As indicated earlier, the poor are a relatively small sector of the subordinate classes, and face the greatest problems of visibility in formal interactions.

16. See p. 35.

17. Studies of the interactional process in welfare offices and in public hospitals serving the poor make this abundantly clear. Frederick Wiseman's film *Welfare* is an especially powerful document in this regard. See also Erving Goffman, *Asylums*.

18. By dominant occupations, we mean those in the professional-managerial class vested with economic, political, and cultural authority. These fall primarily under the Department of Labor's occupational titles of "proprietary" or "professional and managerial." The discussion that follows applies to some degree to the middle-level technical or administrative positions, but mainly to the prestigious professional and top managerial roles occupied primarily by white males of the privileged classes.

19. Students of professionalism have shown that the authority of professionals rests on the claim to hold exclusive specialized knowledge. The authority of managers in the workplace is also legitimated by their exclusive claim to knowledge of the production process. Nicos Poulantzas has argued that differences in knowledge—or, more accurately, claims to knowledge established by educational credentials—serve as the major cultural legitimation of class privileges. The analysis that follows explores this theme in regard to privileges of attention in face-to-face interactions. Poulantzas' general argument is developed in his *Classes in Contemporary Capitalism*.

20. It should be noted that teachers are given direct formal control over the allocation of attention in the classroom. This is institutionalized in the mechanism of hand-raising, which allows the teacher to determine who is the focus of attention at any given moment. In most work settings, those in authority are given the formal power of the chairman over attention in office meetings and other structured interactions at the workplace.

21. The attention-dynamics of the courtroom were highlighted in an unusual fashion during the Vietnam war period in the farcical trial of the "Chicago Seven," when the antiwar defendants refused to abide by normal courtroom ritual and to extend the appropriate respect to Judge Julius Hoffman. Using theatrical techniques, on the one hand, they drew disproportionate attention to themselves and their own political ideas, while also successfully exploiting Hoffman's formally structured "center stage" position and manipulating his visibility to create a notorious symbol of Establishment bigotry and ineptness.

22. This aspect of deference has been explored by Erving Goffman in a number of pioneering essays. See especially "The Nature of Deference and Demeanor" in Goffman, *Interaction Ritual* and *Behavior in Public Places*, pp. 90 ff.

23. Few work roles are purely attention-getting or attention-giving but are a blend of the two, with a greater emphasis on one posture or the other. While the dominant occupational roles have elements of attention-giving, these are being reduced in ways elaborated on pp. 67 ff.

24. In this way, secretaries and other subordinate attention-givers in the work world play an analogous role to dominant groups as domestic servants who, as we have already seen, are hired as attention-givers in the private sphere. In her analysis of the role of the secretary, Mary Benet indicates that her duties approximate those of a wife and servant combined: "She makes his plane reservations, protects him from subordinates, does his expense accounts, sends Christmas cards and listens to his domestic problems." Benet goes on to indicate that in face-to-face interactions with the boss, the secretary takes on a certain kind of invisibility and cannot expect any attention except a flirtatious or sexual kind that she may not desire. The delegation of the attention-giving role thus follows sex-role prescriptions, as secretaries, nurses, and receptionists are typically female while their bosses are characteristically male. See Mary Benet, *The Secretarial Ghetto*, pp. 72 ff.

25. In informal interactions, as Robert Schrank has recently stressed, workers do give and get face-to-face attention from other workers in the "schmoozing" or sociability that is one of the most important and gratifying aspects of work life. Schrank shows, however, that the right to socialize is enjoyed most fully by professionals and others in dominant occupations, as rules, regimentation, and the noise of machines restrict informal interactions among most industrial and clerical workers. See Robert Schrank, *Ten Thousand Working Days*.

26. In the first chapter we defined invisibility as the position of the person in ordinary conversation or any other "focused" face-to-face interaction who receives no attention from others in the interaction. The notion of invisibility is extended here to refer also to those who suffer role-defined exclusion from others with whom they are physically proximate but are not engaged in "focused" face-to-face interaction. This includes workers in "partly focused" interactions who have official status as participants in the situation but are excluded from the conversation or gaze of the others involved. Many of the examples of invisible workers that follow, including the discussion of kitchen help, janitors, and domestics, refer to invisibility in "partly focused" settings and interactions rather than the fully "focused" interactions discussed earlier.

27. Invisibility from the public is a special form of invisibility in "partly focused" settings. It is unique because it involves clear physical separation from others to whom one's services are directed. Other workers, such as busboys, who enter the front region but are not acknowledged, suffer a different kind. They can be physically seen by the public, but are systematically ignored. This second form is discussed further in the paragraph that follows.

28. This form of invisibility is characteristic of all "partly focused" interactions where people such as waiters and cleaners are expected to be physically present but are excluded from the "focused" interaction of the main participants. Since it is only workers of very low status who are assigned the "invisible" position in such settings, this suggests that their invisibility is a symbolic representation of their degraded moral status.

29. Supervisory attention occurs in both "focused" and "partly focused" settings. The worker becomes the focus of supervisory attention in "focused" interactions when the supervisor engages in direct face-to-face talk with him, as when he verbally instructs him or admonishes him. More often, supervisory attention is given in "partly focused" situations, where the supervisor is watching the workers and monitoring their behavior but is not conversing with them or otherwise engaging in "focused" interaction.

30. This reflects the prevailing view of the social order, and the occupational structure specifically, as meritocratic. In a meritocracy, the place on the occupational ladder achieved by each person is understood as a reflection of his own abilities. This perception of the social structure is consistent with the ideology of individualism in contemporary culture and serves to legitimate the class system itself. For a discussion of these issues, see Richard Sennett and Jonathan Cobb, *The Hidden Injuries of Class*.

31. See Peter Trudgill, "Sex, Covert Prestige and Linguistic Change in the Urban British English of Norwich," in Thorne and Henley (eds.), *Language and Society*, pp. 88–104.

32. Members of dominant classes have the greatest resources to pursue higher education and are most likely to do so. Extensive research in the United States has demonstrated this empirical relation between education and class. See especially Jerome Karabel, "Community Colleges and Social Stratification," *Harvard Educational Review*.

33. The ethos of self-development, while conceived by educators such as John Dewey or psychologists such as Carl Rogers as an expression of humanistic culture, thus becomes, in a highly individualistic and competitive society, a means of differentiating and stratifying people. It serves as the basis for a new hierarchy, a form of psychological meritocracy, in which attention and other psychological rewards are allocated to those on top.

34. See William Labov, *Sociolinguistic Patterns; The Social Stratification of English in New York City* (Washington, D.C.: Center for Applied Linguistics, 1966); Roger W. Shuy, Walter A. Wolfram, and William K. Riley, *Linguistic Correlates of Social Stratification in Detroit Speech*.

35. See studies summarized in A. Paul Hare (ed.) *Handbook of Small Group Research* pp. 212 ff.

36. See, for example, P. W. Jackson, *Life in Classrooms*, and Robert Rosenthal and Lenore Jacobson, *Pygmalion in the Classroom*.

Chapter 5

1. See Erich Fromm, *The Sane Society*.
2. As Fromm and others have stressed, this thrusting of the individual "on his own" is at the very heart of social individualism. The individual necessarily feels more vulnerable under these conditions and less protected from danger than in community-centered societies, where he is protected by the group from perils of the environment. As Lasch has recently pointed out, this sense of endangerment is closely associated with the development of self-orientation, and is closely related to the narcissism emerging in the contemporary American character. See Erich Fromm, *Escape From Freedom*, and Christopher Lasch, *The Culture of Narcissism*.
3. For a development of this thesis, see Richard Sennett and Jonathan Cobb, *The Hidden Injuries of Class*.
4. Marx regarded the destruction of community life as an essential concomitant of the expansion of the market place and the growth of private capital. The transfer of ownership and control of economic resources, including land and capital, to capitalist forces outside the traditional community undermined its integrity. Since the communities of medieval society were based on precapitalist forms of domination and oppression, Marx did not mourn their passing. Nonetheless, in his discussion of the capitalist market's brutal reduction of human relations to self-interested calculation and naked self-interest, Marx forecast the weakening of social bonds and the ensuing rise of the disaffiliated "self."

   The Marxist analysis implies an erosion of community in two stages. The first involves the destruction of feudal communities by the rise of competitive capitalism, discussed in the text. The second is the eclipse of the vestiges of community in the small town settings of competitive capitalism by the metropolitization associated with the rise of monopoly capital. Monopolization intensified processes set in motion by the competitive stage, as it removed economic control to mass corporate institutions even further removed from the community and increasingly beyond its control.

   Other social theorists, many not within the Marxist tradition, have also analyzed the demise of community as a consequence of the displacement of economic and other functions to mass institutions, especially the corporation and the state. In his discussions of the social bases of community, Robert Nisbet has forcefully demonstrated that traditional communities survive only by carrying out social, economic, and political functions creating interdependence and meaning among their members. Nisbet emphasizes that a defining characteristic of modern society is the removal of such functions from the community-level institutions of family, neighborhood, and church to corporations and especially the state. See Robert Nisbet, *The Quest for Community* and Karl Marx and Friedrich Engels, *The German Ideology*.
5. In such a culture, the individualistic need to prove one's worth and distinctiveness as an individual is even more evident: it is a culture entirely devoted to the development of individuality. Yet the criterion of individual merit is no longer economic success but the unfolding of the most "creative" and "subtle" facets of the self. See Philip Reiff, *The Triumph of the Therapeutic*.

6. In regard to mental health, the pernicious meaning of excessive individualism was first pointed out by Emile Durkheim. In his famous study of suicide, Durkheim showed that people who live under social conditions of extreme individualism (isolation, lack of community) are particularly prone to a form of suicide he calls egoistic, one in which the individual has become so obsessively preoccupied with himself that it leads to a total rupture of consciousness with the world.

Conclusion to Second Edition

1. Will and Ariel Durant, *The Age of Napoleon*. Vol. 11 of *The Story of Civilization*. NY: Simon and Schuster, 1975, p. 81.
2. The quote from Lord Chesterfield is cited in Will and Ariel Durant, *The Age of Voltaire*. Vol. 9 of *The Story of Civilization*. NY: Simon and Schuster, 1965, p. 81.
3. For a discussion of the transformation of jobs and its impact on character, see Richard Sennett, *The Corrosion of Character: The Personal Consequences of Work in the New Capitalism*. NY: W. W. Norton, 1998. For another discussion, see Charles Derber, *Corporation Nation: How Corporations Are Taking Over Our Lives and What We Can Do About It*. NY: St. Martin's Press, 1998.
4. I conducted these interviews in Boston in 1996. Temporary employment agencies, as well as companies that add their own internal temp pools, provided me with names to contact. I tape-recorded interviews, which typically lasted two hours.
5. For a discussion of job genocide, see Derber, *Corporation Nation*. Op.cit., Chapter 5.
6. See Charles Derber, *The Wilding of America*. NY: St. Martin's Press, 1996.
7. For further discussion, see Ibid., and Sennett, *The Corrosion of Character*. Op.cit.
8. See Mitch Albom, *Tuesdays With Morrie*. NY: Doubleday, 1997.
9. For Morrie's own words on these subjects, see the transcripts from his three Nightline interviews with Ted Koppel, and his own book, Morrie Schwartz, *Morrie: In His Own Words*. NY: Walker and Co., 1999.
10. C. Wright Mills, *The Sociological Imagination*. Op.cit.
11. For a discussion of community-oriented groups and movements, see Jeremy Rifkin, *The End of Work*. NY: Knopf, 1996. See also Derber, *Corporation Nation*. Op.cit., Chapter 15.
12. For a discussion of the new role of unions in a world of disposable labor, see Stanley Aronowitz, *From the Ashes of the Old*. Boston: Houghton Mifflin, 1998. See also Derber, *Corporation Nation*. Op. Cit., Chapter 15.
13. For a discussion of the failure of communitarians to discuss how markets undermine community, see Charles Derber, *What's Left?* Amherst, Mass.: University of Massachusetts Press, 1995, Chapter 9.
14. See Alan Wolfe, *Whose Keeper? Social Science and Moral Obligation*. Berkely, Calif.: University of California Press, 1991.
15. On the spread of markets and market ideology, see Robert Kuttner, *Everything for Sale: The Virtues and Limits of Markets*. NY: Knopf, 1997. See also Derber, *Corporation*

Nation. Op.cit. On the theme of markets and loyalty, see Sennett, *The Corrosion of Character.* Op.cit.

16. For an in-depth discussion of reforms necessary to curb markets and build community, see Derber, *Corporation Nation.* Op.cit., Chapters 10–15.

17. For an elaboration and critique of this kind of corporate responsibility, see Ibid., Chapter 14.

Bibliography

Addeo, E. G., and R. Burger. *Ego Speak*. New York: Bantam, 1973.

Allen, Lucy. *Table Service*. Boston: Little Brown, 1923.

Amory, Cleveland. *The Proper Bostonians*. New York: Dutton, 1948.

Argyle, Michael, Mansur Lallee, and Mark Cook, "The Effects of Visibility on Interaction in the Dyad." *Human Relations*, 21 (1968): 3–17.

Bales, Robert F. *Personality and Social Interaction*. New York: Holt, Rinehart, 1971.

————, and Talcott Parsons. *Family, Socialization, and Interaction Process*. Glencoe, Illinois: Free Press, 1955.

————, and Philip Slater. "Role Differentiation in Small Decision-making Groups." In T. Parson and R. F. Bales *et al.*, *The Family and Interaction Process*. New York: Free Press, 1955, pp. 259–306.

Baltzell, E. Digby. *Philadelphia Gentlemen*. Glencoe, Illinois: The Free Press, 1958.

Bell, Daniel. *The Coming of Post-Industrial Society*. New York: Harper, 1973.

————. *The Cultural Contradictions of Capitalism*. New York: Basic Books, 1976.

Bender, Marilyn. *The Beautiful People*. New York: Coward-McCann, 1967.

Benet, Mary. *The Secretarial Ghetto*. New York: McGraw-Hill, 1972.

Berger, Peter, Brigitte Berger, and H. Keliner. *The Homeless Mind*. New York: Vintage, 1973.

Bernard, Jessie. *The Future of Marriage*. New York: World, 1972.

————. *The Future of Motherhood*. New York: Dial, 1974.

————. "Talk, Conversation, Listening, Silence." In *The Sex Game*. New York: Atheneum, 1972, pp. 153–64.

Birmingham, Stephen. *The Right People*. Boston: Little, Brown, 1958.

Bledstein, Burton J. *The Culture of Professionalism*. New York: Norton, 1976.

Bowlby, John. *Maternal Care and Mental Health*. Geneva: World Health Organization, 1952.

Boyers, Robert (ed.). *Psychological Man*. New York: Harper, 1975.

Braverman, Harry. *Labor and Monopoly Capital*. New York: Monthly Review Press, 1974.

Brenton, Myron. *The American Male*. New York: Fawcett-Premier, 1966.

Britaan, Arthur. *The Privatized World*. London: Routledge, Kegan, Paul, 1977.

Brown, Bruce. *Marx, Freud and the Critique of Everyday Life*. New York: Monthly Review, 1973.

Burke, Thomas. *Dinner Is Served*. London: Butler and Tanner, 1937.

Centers, Richard. *The Psychology of Social Classes*. Princeton, NJ: Princeton University Press, 1949.

Chance, M. R. A., and Ray Larson (eds.). *The Social Structure of Attention*. New York: John Wiley, 1976.

Chessler, Phyllis. *Women and Madness*. New York: Doubleday, 1972.

Chodorow, Nancy. *The Social Reproduction of Mothering*. Berkeley, Calif.: University of California Press, 1977.

Coser, Rose Laug. "Laughter Among Colleagues." *Psychiatry*, 23 (1960): 81–95.

de Beauvoir, Simone. *The Second Sex*. New York: Bantam, 1961. (First published, 1947.)

Derber, Charles. *Corporation Nation*. New York: St. Martins, 1998.

Derber, Charles. *The Wilding of America*. New York: St Martins, 1996.

Durkheim, Émile. *The Division of Labor*. New York: Free Press, 1964.

———. *Suicide*. New York: Free Press, 1951.

Dworkin, Andrea. *Woman-Hating*. New York: Plume, 1991.

Ewen, Stewart. *Captains of Consciousness*. New York: McGraw-Hill, 1976.

Firestone, Shulamith. *The Dialectic of Sex*. New York: Bantam, 1970.

Frederick, Portia, and Carol Towner. *The Office Assistant*. Philadelphia: Saunders, 1956.

Freud, Sigmund. *On Narcissism*. London: Hogarth, 1957.

Friedan, Betty. *The Feminine Mystique*. New York: Dell, 1963.

Fromm, Erich. *Escape From Freedom*. New York: Avon, 1941.

———. *Man For Himself*. New York: Rinehart, 1947.

———. *The Sane Society*. New York: Rinehart and Winston, 1955.

Gerth, Hans, and C. Wright Mills. *Character and Social Structure*. New York: Oxford University Press, 1951.

Goffman, Erving. *Asylums*. New York: Anchor, 1961.

———. *Behavior in Public Places*. New York: Free Press, 1963.

———. *Interaction Ritual*. New York: Anchor, 1967.

———. *The Presentation of Self in Everyday Life*. New York: Anchor, 1959.

———. *Relations in Public*. New York: Harper, 1971.

Goldberg, Steven. *The Inevitability of Patriarchy*. New York: Morrow, 1973.

Gornick, Vivian, and B. K. Moran. *Woman in Sexist Society*. New York: Mentor, 1972.

Greer, Germaine. *The Female Eunuch*. New York: McGraw-Hill, 1971.

Habermas, Jurgen. *Legitimation Crisis*. Boston: Beacon Press, 1975.

Hare, A. Paul (ed.). *Handbook of Small Group Research*. Glencoe, Illinois: Free Press, 1962.

Henry, Jules. *Pathways to Madness*. New York: Vintage, 1965.

Hilpert, Fred, Cheris Kramer, and Ruth Ann Clark, "Participants' Perception of Self and Partner in Mixed-Sex Dyads." *Central States, Speech Journal* (Spring 1975).

Hirschman, Lynette. "Analysis of Supportive and Assertive Behavior in Conversations." Paper presented at Linguistic Society of America, 1974.

———. "Female-Male Differences in Conversational Interaction." Paper presented at Linguistic Society of America, 1973.

Hoch, G. and R. Zubin (eds.). *Psychopathology of Communication*. New York: Grune and Stratton, 1958.

Howe, Louise Kapp. *Pink Collar Workers: Inside the World of Women's Work*. New York: Avon, 1977.

Jaccoby, Russell. *Social Amnesia*. Boston: Beacon Press, 1975.

Jackson, P. W. *Life in Classrooms*. New York: Holt, Rinehart and Winston, 1968.

Josephsons, Erich and Mary (eds.). *Man Alone*. New York: Dell, 1962.

Kahler, Erich. *The Tower and the Abyss*. New York: George Brazillier, 1957.

Karabel, Jerome. "Community Colleges and Social Stratification." *Harvard Educational Review* 42 (November 1972).

Kavaler, Lucy. *The Private Life of High Society*. New York: David McKay, 1960.

Keniston, Kenneth. *The Uncommitted*. New York: Harcourt, Brace & World, 1969.

Kenkel, William F. "Observational Studies of Husband-Wife Interaction Family Decision-Making." In M. Sussman (ed.) *Sourcebook in Marriage and the Family*. Boston: Houghton Mifflin, 1963, pp. 144–56.

Kernberg, Otto. "Factors in the Psychoanalytic Treatment of Narcissistic Personalities." *Journal of American Psychoanalytic Treatment*, 18, 1 (1970): 51–85.

Kohut, Heinz. *The Analysis of the Self*. New York: International University Press, 1971.

Kolko, Gabriel. *Wealth and Power in America*. New York: Praeger, 1962.

Komarovsky, Mirra. *Blue-Collar Marriage*. New York: Vintage, 1967.

Kraemer, Cheris. "Folklinguistics." *Psychology Today*, 8 (June 1974): 82–85.

———. "Sterotypes of Women's Speech: The Word from Cartoons." *Journal of Popular Culture* (1976).

Labov, William. *Sociolinguistic Patterns*. Philadelphia: University of Pennsylvania, 1972.

Laing, R. D. *The Divided Self*. London: Penguin, 1965.

Lasch, Christopher. *The Culture of Narcissism*. New York: Basic Books, 1978; revised, NY: Norton, 1991.

———. *Haven in a Troubled World*. New York: Basic Books, 1978.

———. "Narcissistic America." *New York Review of Books*, 22, 15 (September 1976): pp. 5–13.

Lefebvre, Henri. *Everyday Life in the Modern World*. London: Penguin, 1971.

Luckmann, Thomas and Peter Berger. "Social Mobility and Personal Identity." *European Journal of Sociology*, 5 (1964).

Lukacs, Georg. *History and Class-Consciousness*. Cambridge, Mass.: MIT, 1971.

Lukes, Steven. *Individualism*. New York: Harper & Row, 1975.

Malcolm, Henry. *Generation of Narcissus*. Boston: Little, Brown, 1971.

Marcuse, Herbert. *One-Dimensional Man*. Boston: Beacon Press, 1964.

Marx, Karl. *Capital*. Volume 1. Translated by Samuel Moore and Edward Aveling. New York: Modern Library; first published 1906.

———. and Friedrich Engels. *The German Ideology*. Moscow: Foreign Languages Publishing House, 1964.

Mills, C. Wright. *The Power Elite*. New York: Oxford University Press, 1956.

———. *The Sociological Imagination*. New York: Oxford University Press, 1959.

———. *White-Collar*. New York: Oxford University Press, 1951.

Nisbet, Robert. *The Quest for Community*. New York: Oxford University Press, 1955.

Packard, Vance. *A Nation of Strangers*. New York: Pocket Books, 1974.

Parker, Angele. "Sex Differences in Classroom Intellectual Argumentation." M.S. thesis, Penn. State Univ., 1973.

Parker, Richard. *The Myth of the Middle Class*. New York: Harper & Row, 1972.

Pawley, Martin. *The Private Future*. New York: Pocket Books, 1977.

Piaget, Jean. *The Language and Thought of the Child*. New York: New American Library, 1974.

Pleck, Joseph and Jack Sawyer. *Men and Masculinity*. New York: Spectrum, 1974.

Post, Emily. *Etiquette*. New York: Funk and Wagnalls, 1973.

Poulantzas, Nicos. *Classes in Contemporary Capitalism*. London: New Left Books, 1975.

Reich, Wilhelm. *The Mass Psychology of Fascism*. New York: Noonday, 1970.

Reiff, Philip. *Fellow Teachers*. New York: Harper, 1973.

———. *The Triumph of the Therapeutic*. New York: Harper & Row, 1966.

Riesman, David, Nathan Glazer, and Ruell Denny. *The Lonely Crowd*. New Haven, Conn.: Yale University Press, 1950.

Rohman, Mary. "Conversations: Male and Female Experience." Mimeographed, Boston, 1975.

Rosenthal, Robert, and Lenore Jacobson. *Pygmalion in the Classroom*. New York: Holt, Rinehart and Winston, 1968.

Rowbatham, Sheila. *Woman's Consciousness; Man's World*. London: Pelican, 1974.

Schaar, John. *Escape From Authority: The Perspectives of Erich Fromm*. New York: Harper, 1964.

Schrank, Robert. *Ten Thousand Working Days*. Cambridge, Mass.: MIT Press, 1978.

Schroyer, Trent. *The Critique of Domination*. New York: George Brazillier, 1973.

Sennett, Richard. *The Fall of Public Man*. New York: Knopf, 1977.

———. *The Uses of Disorder*. New York: Vintage. 1970.

———. (ed.). *Classic Essays on the Culture of Cities*. New York: Meredith 1969.

———, and Jonathan Cobb. *The Hidden Injuries of Class*. New York: Knopf, 1973.

[Seventeen Magazine]. *The New Seventeen Book of Young Living*. New York: Houpt, 1970.

Shuy, Roger, Walter A. Wolfram, and William K. Riley, *Linguistic Correlates of Social Stratification in Detroit Speech*. Final Report, Project 6–1347. Washington, D.C.: U.S. Office of Education, 1967.

Simmel, Georg. *The Sociology of Georg Simmel*, K. Wolff (ed.). New York: Free Press, 1950.

Slater, Philip. "Culture, Sexuality, and Narcissism." In his *Footholds: Understanding the Shifting Family and Sexual Tensions in Our Culture*. New York: Dutton, 1977.

———. *Earthwalk*. New York: Doubleday, 1974.

———. *The Pursuit of Loneliness*. Boston: Beacon Press, 1970.

Soskin, William and Vera P. John. "The Study of Spontaneous Talk." In Roger Barker (ed.), *The Stream of Behavior*. New York: Appleton-Century-Crofts, 1963.

Spitz, René. "Anaclitic Depression." *Psychoanalytic Study of the Child* 2 (1946): 313–42.

Strodtbeck, Fred. "Husband-Wife Interaction over Revealed Differences." *American Sociological Review*, 16 (1951): 468–73.

———, and Richard Mann. "Sex-Role Differentiation in Jury Deliberations." *Sociometry*, 19 (1956): 3–11.

———, et al. "Social Status in Jury Deliberations." *American Sociological Review*, 22(1957): 713–19.

Tepperman, Jean. *Not Servants, Not Machines: Office-Workers Speak Out*. Boston: Beacon Press, 1976.

Terkel, Studs. *Working*. New York: Avon, 1972.

Thorne, Barrie. "Women in the Draft Resistance Movement: A Case Study of Sex-Roles and Social Movements." *Sex-Roles: A Journal of Research*, 1, 2 (1975).

———, and Nancy Henley (eds.). *Language and Sex*. Rowley, Mass.: Newbury House Publishers, 1975.

Toennies, Frederick. *Community and Society*. East Lansing, Michigan: Michigan State University Press, 1957.

Trudgill, Peter. "Sex, Covert Prestige and Linguistic Change in the Urban British English of Norwich." In *Language and Society*. Cambridge: Cambridge University Press, 1972, pp. 179–95.

Turnbull, Colin. *The Mountain People*. New York: Touchstone, 1972.

Vaughan, W. and E. McGinnies. "Some Biographical Determiners of Participation in Group Discussion." *Journal of Applied Psychology* 41 (1957): 179–85.

Veblen, Thorstein. *The Portable Veblen*, edited by Max Lerner. New York: Viking, 1948.

———. *The Theory of the Leisure Class*. New York: Penguin Classics, 1994.

Weber, Max. *Economy and Society*, edited by G. Roth and C. Wittich. New York: Bedminster Press, 1968.

Whyte, William. *Men at Work*. Homewood, Illinois: Dorsey Press, 1961.

Wilde, Oscar. *The Fairy Tales of Oscar Wilde*. New York: Hart, 1975.

Wirth, Louis. *On Cities and Social Life*, edited by A. J. Reiss, Chicago: University of Chicago Press, 1964.

Zaretsky, Eli. *Capitalism, The Family and Personal Life*. New York: Harper, 1974.

Zimmerman, Don H. and Candace West. "Sex-Roles, Interruptions and Silences in Conversation." In Barrie Thorne and Nancy Henley (eds.), *Language and Sex*. Rowley, Mass.: Newbury House Press, 1975, pp. 105–129.

Index

Ability: badges of, 58, 73–74; as measure of worth, 73; related to education, 75–76

Advertising, 64

Aggressiveness, 12; masculine, 48

Aloneness: under capitalist system, 79–80; need for attention and, 80; related to self-orientation, 80–81

Anxious class, 92–93

Attention: allocation of, 2, 12, 35–37; character and, 44–49; civil, 13, 47, 93, 101; as commodity, 59–62; commonly focused, 10; competition for, 2, 12; displays of knowledge and, 75–77; distribution of, 85–86; education and, 75–77; exchange of, 107*n;* historic pursuit of, 89–90; in the home, 62; in marriage, 95; purchase of, 62–66; purchase of, in therapy, 37, 59–60, 96; in restaurants, 60–62; scarcity of, 109*n;* and social structure, *xxiv–xxvi;* speech and, 76; supervisory, 120*n;* trends in pursuit of, *xiii–xix;* work roles and, 66–74

Attention-dynamics: observations of, 106*n;* shaping of, *xiii*

Attention-Interaction Project. *See* Methodology

Authority: attention and, 42; male character and, 41–42, 48

Automobiles, 64, 118*n*

Background acknowledgments, 27, 29–30, 112*n*

Bales, Robert, 40–41

Barr, Bob, *xxii*

Behavior: economic, 14; formal, 2, 106*n;* informal, 2–3

Benet, Mary, 119*n*

Bernard, Jessie, 38, 40, 51, 113*n*

Bonsignore, Michael, *xx*

Bowlby, John, 9

Buber, Martin, 98

Capitalism: classic model of, 14–15; destruction of community by, 91–92, 102; economic individualism and, 82; influence of, on personal relations, 79; selling of attention under, 62–66, 117*n;* structure of social character under, 110*n*

Change: personal, 99–100; social, 79, 88, 98–103

Character, 110*n*

Chesterfield, Lord, 89

Children: care of, 86–87; civil society and, 101; interaction with mother, 38–40, 107*n,* 113*n*

Civil attention, 13, 47, 101; invisibility and, 93

Civil society, 100–101

Class, anxious, 92–96. *See also* Social class

Classroom: allocation of attention in, 35, 66–67, 69, 118*n;* formal interaction in, 35

Clinton, Bill, *xxiii*

Clothing, and attention-getting, 63–64

Cobb, Jonathan, 120*n*